COMMENTS ON THE CYCLING PERSON

PETER BUCKLEY

Empire Games Road Race Champion

This book is so comprehensive it could be termed the 'Encyclopedia of Cycling'. I cannot think of anyone connected with the sport who would not find his particular aspect covered in this magnificent book. Not only is the book indispensable to the beginner, but the experienced rider will find, as I have, that it is irreplaceable as a book of reference. I can only hope that this book is widely read and foresee, if the information it contains is acted upon, cycling in this country becoming generally recognised as the 'king of sports'.

LES WEST

Twice winner of the Tour of Britain, 2nd Amateur World Road Race Championship

After reading this book, I wished I was back at the start of my cycling career; for the information that I could have obtained from it would have made me a better rider than I am now. I have had to learn the hard way. Right from the first to the last chapter every aspect of road racing is covered in the greatest detail. Every cyclist and keen sportsman will be the poorer without this book on their shelves.

COLIN LEWIS

British Professional Champion and Tour de France rider

I have had to learn about training, diet, position etc., the hard way, coupled with a lot of suffering. Now with a book such as this, written by a rider of the calibre of Peter Ward, all who inspire to be road champions should find the road to the top quicker than I and most of my colleagues have found it. Everyone, from the novice to the hardened veteran, from the would-be sponsor, to race organiser, can learn something of value from this book. All the *King of Sports* readers will come to realize that this sport is indeed the hardest but the most worthwhile of them all.

J. B. WADLEY

Editor of *Sporting Cyclist*

'Can you please recommend a book to me, written in English, dealing with every aspect of cycle racing?'

As editor of a cycling magazine I am constantly getting requests of this kind from all over the world. Until now I have had to reply that such a publication does not exist, although there are plenty in other European languages. Now, Pete Ward has fulfilled a long felt want by writing this book. It is a valuable contribution to the sport; it will help not only the newcomers, but will interest and command the attention of experienced riders and officials as well.

ALAN GAYFER

Editor of *Cycling*

Reading this book I have been refreshed to see that it has the genuine feel of having been written by a bike rider. Too often, it seems, books of this nature have been strung together by half informed writers in fancy English that means little to the youngster trying to learn. Pete is no half-informed writer, but a man who has been through every mill road racing has to offer, and yet who still feels he can learn. Because of this, he has an innate sympathy with the newcomer which communicates itself through each chapter of a long, fascinating book. Any aspiring World road champion would do well to read, mark, learn and inwardly digest this book first.

EDDY SOENS

An England Team Manager

At last, racing cyclists in this country have an authoritative book to guide them to success. As the mentor of several of the countries leading riders, past and present, I know that had my proteges had this book I would have been saved hours of work. Many of the England teams I have directed would have riden far better had they been able to follow the advice contained in *King of Sports*. With a long experience of all aspects of cycle sport, I believe that if both riders and officials carefully consider the advice contained herein, our sport will flourish and prosper.

KING OF SPORTS
CYCLE ROAD RACING

King of Sports: Cycle Road Racing by Peter Ward
PP005

Pendle Press
6 Gellatly Road, London, SE14 5TT, UK

First published in Great Britain in 2024

Designed by Luke Pajak

Copyright © The Ward Family, 2024

Peter Ward has asserted his right under the Copyright, Designs and Patents Act, 1988, to be identified as the author of this work.

All rights reserved. No part of this publication may be reproduced or transmitted in any form or by any means, electronic or mechanical, including photocopying, recording, or any information storage or retrieval system, without prior permission in writing from the publishers.

A catalogue record for this book is available from the British Library.

ISBN - 9781838369323

Printed by Interak, Poland

MIX
Paper from responsible sources
FSC® C105618

PENDLE PRESS

KING OF SPORTS
CYCLE ROAD RACING

BY PETER WARD MBE

The Bollington Road Race 1952, Peter's first race

CONTENTS

List of Illustrations — 10
About the Author — 13
Foreword — 17
Introduction — 21
Cycling Terminology — 24

1. Training — 27
2. Morning and Evening Exercises — 38
3. Massage — 45
4. Diet — 47
5. Clothing — 53
6. Mechanical Equipment — 59
7. Preparation — 66
8. Good Sportsmanship — 71
9. Tactics — 83
10. Stage Events — 99
11. Preparing to Ride in a Stage Race — 107
12. Race Organising — 117
13. Cycling Clubs — 129
14. The Manufacturers — 142
15. Comrades — 145
16. The Legend in Action — 150
17. Three of my Most Memorable Events — 153

Publisher's Note — 159
Recommended Books — 160

KING OF SPORTS

LIST OF ILLUSTRATIONS

p8　　*The Bollington Road Race 1952 – Peter Ward's first cycle race.*
　　　(Ward family)

p12　*Peter Ward, National Championships 1956.*
　　　(Ward family)

p14　*Peter Ward winning the Tour of Britain stage at Morecambe taking the Yellow Jersey, 1956.*
　　　(Ward family)

p15　*'A winning smile. We're proud of you' - a message written by Peter's mum on the back on this photo.*
　　　(Ward family)

p18　*Brian Cookson winning the Lakeland Division Championship in 1971.*
　　　(Brian Cookson)

p20　*Peter Ward crossing the line victorious.*
　　　(Ward family)

p23　*Peter Ward racing.*
　　　(Ward family)

p26　*Jacques Anquetil riding in the 1962 Tour de France, the first cyclist to win the Tour five times.*
　　　(ddsiple, Flickr)

p37　*Peter Ward racing against Alan Jackson in the National Championships 1956.*
　　　(Ward family)

p58　*Randy Alsop (left) and Peter Ward (right) heading out for a training ride in 1956.*
　　　(Ward family)

KING OF SPORTS

p70 Bill Bradley, Peter Ward and Eric Wilson at the Lakeland Division Championships 1957.
(Ward family)

p98 Tommy Simpson becomes World Champion, 1965.
(cycling archives)

p113 Felice Gimondi at the 1969 Giro dell'Appennino.
(Dreamstime)

p144 Beryl Burton OBE competing on the track in 1967 at the World Cycling Championships. That same year she set a new 12-hour time trial record of 277.25 miles – a mark that surpassed the men's record of the time by 0.73 miles and was not superseded by a man until 1969.
(Ron Kroon, ANeFo, CCO)

p149 The Championissimo, Fausto Coppi, at the 1953 Giro d'Italia.
(Wikipedia)

p148 The Grand Prix of Leyland 1969. Peter Ward (left) is wearing clipless pedals, while Peter Matthews (right) has toe clip pedals like most cyclists at the time.
(Ward family)

p158 Peter Ward, front far right, with his father Harry holding Peter's son Dave next to him in the crowd. At that time Peter was the Lakeland Divisional Champion.
(Ward family)

Peter Ward, National Championships 1956

KING OF SPORTS
ABOUT THE AUTHOR

Peter was a dynamic character who believed nothing was impossible. A former international cyclist, he began cycling at the age of 16, often borrowing a bike to go out on club runs. Initially he joined Leyland Clarion Cycling Club, before he and four other cyclists formed The Ribble Valley Cycling Club in 1951. Shortly after Peter won his first race at the age of 18, wearing a football shirt with a blue band stitched across the front.

Nothing could stop Peter's competitive spirit. When he was conscripted to do his National Service in the RAF, posted to the South of England, he would ride home to Lostock Hall to see his future wife Nora Critchley and back to barracks in a weekend. Luckily the RAF spotted Peter's talent for racing in a televised event and from then on gave him all the privileges of riding for the RAF team.

Peter's time in the RAF led him to become an engineer at British Aerospace, at both Warton and Strand Road sites, a job he never tired of. He continued racing to an international level, riding for England during the 50s and 60s. His proudest moment was winning the stage into Morecambe in the 1956 Tour of Britain, Peter enjoyed bringing the yellow jersey home to Lancashire.

Peter won over 30 first class races and organised many top-class racing events including the International Grand Prix of Leyland, an 80-mile gruelling road race attracting some of the top UK and European road cyclists. Once described as the 'Sterling Moss' of cycle racing as both sportsmen were notorious for racing hard and crashing often! Peter's racing history leaves a captivating list of events:

1955 – In the Amateur Circuit of Britain, away in a leading group of riders on the next to the last stage and race leader on the road, he was brought off his cycle by the leading riders' team car.

1956 – Peter finished four seconds behind Ericol Baldini in the Isle of Man International. Won the National Championships but was disqualified. Crashed and broke his wrist in the Tour Sweden.

KING OF SPORTS

1957 – In the National Championships, Peter finished fourth. After being in a breakaway for 100 miles he was caught four miles from the finish.

1959 – In the Tour of Britain, in 7th position, his forks broke, on the only part of the whole 1,000 mile course that service cars were instructed to by-pass. He then devoted his energies to the team. This regional team, at the finish, beat all the national teams and had riders in 1st, 4th and 8th positions.

1961 – Peter crashed on the 7th stage, when lying in fourth position in the Tour of Britain.

1962 – In the London to Holyhead 257 mile race, Peter was leading 8 riders away, with half a mile to go, John Geddes' crank broke and he fell in front of Peter, causing him to crash.

1967 – A week after winning the Players No. 6 1st Category event he was brought off accidentally and fractured his pelvis.

The 1967 crash led Peter, whilst recovering from injury, to write this iconic cycling handbook *The King of Sports*, termed the 'Encyclopaedia of cycling' by international cyclist Les West, and the book was sold throughout the world.

Peter Ward winning the Tour of Britain stage at Morecambe taking the Yellow Jersey, 1956.

ABOUT THE AUTHOR

Peter used to cycle a round trip of 24 miles to work at BAE, virtually every day throughout his working life. After retirement he continued to instigate and be involved in creating new safer cycling routes to BAE systems. His idea of establishing a comprehensive cycle route network in Lancashire, led to him to become the architect of the iconic Guild Wheel. Peter spent years developing the 21-mile orbital greenway around the city, providing safe, scenic and healthy cycling around Preston. His dream was realised in 2012. Now over 100,000 people a year use the Guild Wheel for walking, running, cycling and commuting to work or school. It provides a safe route for the most vulnerable road users.

Peter served as an elected Labour City Councillor for over 30 years, including Chair of Housing, tackling deprivation, health issues, poverty and other inequalities.

Peter became a Trade Union representative at British Aerospace for the Warton site. Eventually, he was elected as National President of Trade Union TASS (now Unite), enabling him to play a major role in campaigning for workers' rights. He was elected as Trustee of BAE Pension fund and worked tirelessly for better pensions for his fellow workers. Peter's knowledge and experience led him to writing the book, The Great British Pensions Robbery. Barbara Castle wrote this was of 'special importance to women.'

'A winning smile. We're proud of you' - a message written by Peter's mum on the back on this photo.

Peter served as a Justice of the Peace at Preston Magistrates Court for over 40 years. He was made a Guild Burgess in 2012 and had been involved in recent Preston Guilds, including commissioning in 1992 the sculpture of the 1842 martyrs outside Preston's Corn Exchange. The placing of the memorial is a reminder now and in the future that, 'Never without sacrifice, have gains been made towards justice and democracy.' In 2012 Peter was awarded an MBE for his services to cycling. His legacy, the highly acclaimed Guild Wheel, took 12 years to come into fruition and is embraced by the people of Preston as the 'Jewel in Preston's crown.'

Brian Cookson, former President of Union Cycliste International (UCI), described Peter as one of the most influential people in his life recalling, 'We had great times on the bike, training and racing, and many fascinating discussions on the way. Those were part of my formative years and I will never forget them. Quite simply Pete helped me raise my aspirations in life because he always had the attitude that if you wanted something improved or changed then it was up to you to contribute to that change. So, I can say in all honesty that I would never have begun the journey that led to me becoming UCI president if I hadn't known Pete. For me it was a privilege to have known him.'

Peter Ward sadly died in 2017, five years after the Guild Wheel was opened. In 2021 a memorial to Peter was created on the Guild Wheel near Fernyhalgh Lane, it is called Peter's Garden.

Peter's Garden is a natural wildflower garden with trees, benches and a granite stone plaque in memory.

Preston City Mayor Javed Iqbal said at the opening ceremony, 'I am truly honoured to open this fitting memorial to Peter Ward. A man who's passion for cycling knew no bounds'.

KING OF SPORTS

FOREWORD

I was delighted to be asked to write the Foreword for this new edition of *King of Sports* by Peter Ward. It is perhaps difficult to imagine, in this era when books about cycling are so numerous and ubiquitous, that this book, first published in 1968, was in fact the first book in the English language on the subject of cycle road racing - its tactics, how to train for it, and how it should be organised. It was ground–breaking at the time.

When I first joined a cycling club, in 1965 in Preston, Lancashire, having been inspired by the remarkable victory of Tom Simpson in the World Road Championships that year, Pete was a local hero. His formidable training rides were legendary and his performances at national level were talked about with awe. When, after a few months with the local group of the Cyclists Touring Club, I started to think about racing and graduated to training with the 'chaingang' of local racing clubs Ribble Valley CRC and Preston Wheelers, Pete was very much the leader of the group. We all looked to him as a role model.

When his book was published, we found it contained much of the advice and many of the anecdotes which he shared with us – on the bikes, and at café stops on long winter rides. Plus much more details, facts, and examples from his lived experiences. As I progressed from junior to senior ranks, and raced in events alongside him, I not only saw him applying this accrued expertise, but also learned from him in pre and post-race discussions, as he often generously gave me a lift to and from those events.

In fact, it was often during those journeys or on training weekends on the tough roads of Lancashire and the Lake District that I learned other things from Pete – about health and fitness generally, about how to organise cycling events of course, but also about ethics and integrity, about politics and about the ways of the world.

I learned from Pete that if you weren't happy about something, if you wanted to make something happen, if you wanted to change the world, or just change the bits of it that affected you, then there was no point waiting for other people, you had to get involved. Outside the world of cycling as well, Pete demonstrated all of those qualities in his own life, in trade unionism, in politics and as a magistrate. And of course, through his family, and through his relationships with friends and colleagues.

For me, learning from that example led to organising races when I felt there was a shortage of the kind of events that were needed, then becoming a local official of the then British Cycling Federation, then a national official, then an international official, then President of British Cycling, before finally being elected as President of the UCI (Union Cycliste Internationale), cycling's international governing body. All whilst continuing to enjoy regularly riding my bike and competing in cycle races, as and when family, career and other demands on my time permitted.

So, Pete's impact on me, particularly during those formative years of my late teens and early twenties, was both considerable and long-lasting. Perhaps not surprisingly, I've kept my original copy of *King of Sports* on my shelves all those years. Reading it again today half a century later, though obviously of its time, it remains remarkably relevant and useful. Any current rider or follower of modern cycle racing will, I'm sure, learn something new and will be charmed and enthused by reading it today.

BRIAN COOKSON

Brian Cookson winning the Lakeland Division Championship in 1971.

Peter Ward crossing the line victorious.

KING OF SPORTS
INTRODUCTION

Cycle road racing is one of the greatest, if not the greatest, of sports. It has been classed as one of the three most grueling sports along with cross-channel swimming and marathon running. But these two events do not compare with cycle racing for speed, tactics and excitement. Many sports editors and columnists, most of the general public, and the majority of cyclists do not know what it is all about. I hope this book will enable them to appreciate this superb sport.

There is no other book in the English language entirely devoted to describing this complex sport. I thought it was high time we had one.

It has taken me over fifteen years to gain the knowledge and experience in this book—some of it learned through errors which have lost me many prizes, some through long association with top-class riders, athletes in other sports and reading many books on the training of athletes.

I hope that many ambitious newcomers to the sport can progress more quickly, now that they have this guide, than I and many racing colleagues were able to do without one.

Even now after twenty years of road racing experience in this country I see riders of international class making mistakes a coached junior would not make on the Continent. It is high time we improved. I think I can show the way, not only to the uncoached rider, but to many of the big-hearted yet misguided officials who run this sport.

I have covered all aspects of cycling that come into contact with road racing because many of these are integral to the game.

In my paragraphs about racing and training, I have described the methods, in detail, for the young athlete who wishes to become a champion. This does not mean that I have no time for those preoccupied with studies, parents juggling family life, the veteran, or anyone who just likes to have a try. Our sport is big enough to accommodate all. But it is obvious that these latter people do not need, or cannot put into practice, all I have suggested, but they can pick out of this book whatever they have time to utilise. The diet, breathing and daily exercise will help everyone to achieve a healthier life.

To the younger riders I would like to say this: learn to like cycling for itself, for the beautiful countryside you see, for the good companionship and for the health, economy and peacefulness. From the elation you feel at the view from the top of a big hill you have climbed to the scalp-tingling speed of the descent. Cycling can be all fun, all adventure. It can bring personal achievement and fitness that can never be found in a stuffy car or on a noisy motor scooter.

Not enough thought is given to the subject of fitness in later life. Many of the forty plus cyclists give the answer. Their healthy lungs and supple limbs are a glowing example to many of their short winded, lethargic contemporaries.

Unless I go out on my cycle at least twice a week I become pent up and feel like exploding. I am sure that for man, the ex-hunter, it is not natural or healthy to potter round the coffee bar or house.

Teenagers who start street fights or damage property are often physically keyed up. An athlete unwinds in training or competition. I have yet to meet a racing cyclist who is a thug.

So I feel it is in the interest of society to encourage this sport as an outlet for man's natural aggressiveness, nationally and internationally.

PETER WARD

Peter Ward racing.

KING OF SPORTS
CYCLING TERMINOLOGY

Position: The rider's outline when riding.

On the tops: To ride with the hands on the top part of the handlebars.

On the drops, hooks or bottoms: Hand on the bottom part of the handlebars.

Honk: To climb out of the saddle by standing on the pedals.

On the left, on the right, below: Shout given by riders at the front warning riders behind of the positions of obstructions on the road.

Brakes: Warning shouted by riders in front to warn riders behind to stop or to slow rapidly.

Sit on a wheel, shelter, be paced: To ride close behind another rider allowing him to break the wind.

Bit and bit: Each rider after doing a short period at the front (breaking the wind) moves to one side and is overtaken by the rider behind him who does likewise. Each overtaken rider drops back and joins on the tail end of the group.

Echelon: Riders staggered behind each other to protect each other from a cross wind.

Breakaway, break, leading group: Group or groups of riders in front of the main group.

Bunch, pack, field: The largest group of riders in the race.

To attack, to jump: Title given to a rider or group of riders trying to pull away from a group or individual.

CYCLING TERMINOLOGY

To defend: A rider or group of riders who try to slow down a bunch or break away to protect a teammate.

Burned off, dropped, off the back: those who are left behind during the race.

Bonk: Weak through exhaustion.

Hunger knock: Weak through hunger.

Domestic: A lower placed member of a team who works for his team leader.

Primes: Used to stimulate the racing by offering prizes to the first rider past various points on the course.

Half wheeling: Some silly riders when out training try to keep half a wheel in front of the rider alongside. When the lagging rider closes the gap, the leading rider goes faster so that the pace builds up and up. A silly practice.

Bridge the gap: A rider or a small group who leave a larger group and speed across the space between to join a leading group or individual.

Independent: A semi-professional rider.

Sponsor: Financial backing, usually as advertising, to pay a team or individual's expenses, or to provide financial support for a race.

Jacques Anquetil riding in the 1962 Tour de France, the first cyclist to win the Tour five times.

CHAPTER 1

TRAINING

I have started with Training because this is fundamental. The best equipment, massage, tactics and dieting will be wasted unless the rider gets down to this all-important task early in the year.

TRAINING SCHEDULE

Routine and encouragement are two important factors to induce a rider to train. Routine is best served by deciding with your teammates, if possible, during December how you are going to train. Note this in your diary and stick to this routine until you start racing. A graph is a good guide, starting at about 50 miles the first week in January and continuing a straight line to 320 miles per week by the second week in March. Even though you may not feel like going out on your appointed days, do so, unless the roads are icy, it is raining heavily, or you are ill. Only if you still feel 'off' after 5 miles call it a day.

Encouragement is given by good, keen teammates, well-attended training runs, a good trainer, interested parents or partner and a good club. It is grand to be encouraged and I know quite a few couldn't-care-less riders who have been pushed to the top by enthusiastic followers. It is difficult not to turn out for a run if you know that your teammates are waiting, or your trainer arrives with a moped revving for the off. Although, remember many a dedicated athlete has made the grade without these spurs to success.

Here is my suggested 'prior to racing' training schedule. Generally, riders of small or frail build will do less, riders of very heavy build, more, and juniors and ladies approximately two-thirds of the distance stated.

NOVEMBER-DECEMBER

Steady club runs on Sunday. Enjoy the companionship and the scenery. Start physically attuning the whole of your body in the gym and/or at home. Circuit training is ideal. I prefer a gym where games like basketball and touch rugby are also played. I expend myself more when enjoying myself in competition than by trying to be enthusiastic at a rather monotonous sport like weight training.

If you have suitable weights available, start the routine detailed later on in the book every other day, building up the weights as you gain strength. Running is an excellent way to increase your lung capacity.

Do the early morning and evening exercises I describe later. Eat sensibly and get at least eight hours sleep per night.

Have a medical and dental check-up. Arrange with your doctor to give you a course of anti-tetanus injections, to safeguard you should you crash during the season. All international and regional team managers should insist on this being done for all riders under their care.

Training is hard enough and the excuse 'I cannot go as fast on my heavy bike' is poor and the wrong psychological approach.

Keep your cycle as light as possible. Make sure it is kept clean and roadworthy. Do not keep your club mates and yourself shivering while you keep stopping with trouble. Use mudguards, carry a waterproof jacket and some good tools.

TRAINING – EARLY SEASON LONG RUNS

Keep these runs brisk but not aggressive; no half wheeling. Juniors and Internationals, if in the same club, should be able to ride the first few runs together.

Ride two abreast and keep changing the riders at the front every half mile if your group is large, or every mile if it is small. One way is to change in twos, both front riders singling up on the near side. The club overtakes them and the two then join on the back. Another method is to let the outside leader overtake his inside companion and move in front of him, then all the outside riders move up two places.

If you are fit then make your periods at the front a bit longer, but not so fast that you split the group up. Should you be unfit, only stay at the front for a short time, and if you are really tired, stay at the back all the time.

When you are riding well don't shout at some chap at the back: 'Come on and work', and then sprint off to show him. If he is idling—so what! You are training—not racing for big money. If he is unfit and you 'drop' him, you will not have encouraged him to attain fitness.

TRAINING

Similarly, if you are unfit do not overtire yourself by trying to do your share at the front. Do short spells and when you are tired rest at the back until you recuperate. Don't be left exhausted on your own, about 40 miles from home. Try harder each week until you are 'on form'.

At the top of a long climb the leaders should not wait around shivering, but should ride back down and encourage the stragglers. Similarly, when a rider punctures or has some other trouble one rider should stay with him, the other riders should carry on for a couple of miles and then turn back to meet the delayed riders.

If your club is big enough then organise two or three training groups with about ten or twelve matched riders in each group. If you are new to a club do not be over-confident, but join a group you think you can manage. Do not show them how good you are at the beginning and get dropped before the end of the run.

When your club is small, then drop the juniors and unfit riders after 20 miles at a pre-arranged place, or arrange to meet them on the way back. This keeps the club together and encourages new riders.

On Sundays take a spare vest and thick shirt. Change into them if you stop for lunch. Most of the continentals train non-stop. To stop and chat over a cup of tea is part of our cycling tradition. I therefore suggest, if you prefer to stop, only stop once between ten and twenty miles from home. This means your training is over and after your meal you can potter home with the rest of the club.

When your distances are over 60 miles you can carry food and one bottle of liquid refreshment. Take a few extra biscuits or sandwiches as it is far better to arrive home with them in your musette than to die of hunger 20 miles from home. Your body's reserves are ample for training under 60 miles.

During late February and early March, try and get in two or three long weekends. Start out Friday evening to a bed and breakfast place about 60 miles from home. Train from the H.Q. on Saturday, and on Sunday take a roundabout route home. This gives a break from routine, new training country and a step up in terms of miles.

TRAINING – EVENINGS AND SHORT RUNS

Company makes dark evenings more pleasant, and if all members have good lights, it is safer. A good light is essential, as a sudden bend or pothole is upon you before you realise it on a dark night.

I was once training in the dark and luckily spotted the road had subsided 40 feet into a quarry.

A good rear light is also vital. Many cyclists have been hurt at night through dim rear lights. The silly single cell rear light strapped to the saddle is asking for trouble. I prefer to fix my big rear light, with reflector incorporated, to the back wheel spindle area, so that a glance between my legs assures me it is on. Always carry spare bulbs.

On dark evenings try to find a quiet, well-illuminated circuit. I think the fluorescent jackets worn by motorway workmen would be ideal for making cyclists conspicuous and therefore safer in the dark.

If you are using high pressure tyres then carry a spare inner tube. It could save you trying to find a slow puncture on a dark, cold night.

Use a reasonably flat circuit, about two miles round on uncrowded country roads when the evenings are lighter. Use this circuit all the time for your short fast evenings and let all clubs join in unless there are too many. Ride your short training runs in echelon. The younger and unfit riders can miss a lap every so often by riding steadily the opposite way and then, when rested, join in again. This gives hard work for the fit men who are constantly riding against refreshed opposition. It also encourages the others and teaches the inexperienced how to ride as they should in road races.

Keep your training groups compact, six to ten riders is ideal. Larger formations are unwieldy and can be dangerous; usually the bigger the group the less work per rider.

Have three or four primes and a finishing sprint on the course. Allow yourself a 5 mile warming down period at the end of your session.

Before you start to race, ensure you have practiced riding in echelon, whichever way the wind is blowing: figs. 1, 2, 3 & 4 illustrate. When the wind or course changes direction, you should change your position behind the man in front (not forgetting to inform him you have done so).

On your longer evening runs you should still meet your companions riding

TRAINING

on the small circuits. Those who wish to do more miles can arrive early and do a few extra laps. Riders will not need to stand around waiting for the late arrivals. When you are ready you can move off onto a bigger circuit for a change of terrain and scenery.

Interval training is used in many sports and the eastern bloc countries have applied it successfully to cycle racing. Generally, the idea is to simulate racing effort without racing fatigue. Using a small circuit, warm up for five miles, then alternate these two speeds: flat out for half a mile, easy (14 mph) for half a mile, and so on, until you have covered 5, 10 or 15 miles depending on your fitness. During the slow periods, breathe deeply and try to get your pulse rate nearly normal before sprinting again. Cool down by riding steadily home.

After runs, sit quietly by the fire, well wrapped up with a towel round your head, until you have stopped perspiring. Where a bath or shower is not possible, always have a rub down and wipe between your legs with surgical spirit. Change your clothes—do not stand about in sweaty garments.

TRAINING SCHEDULE

	\multicolumn{15}{c	}{SUGGESTED DAILY TRAINING SCHEDULE (MEDIUM-HEAVY RIDERS)}
SUN	F 50 ESY	F 60 ESY	F 70 ESY	U 75 MED	U 80 MED	H 85 MED	F 95 MED	U 100 MED	H 110 MED	F 120 MED	U 120 MED	U 130 MED	RAC	RAC	RAC
MON	GYM	GYM	GYM	GYM	GYM	GYM	GYM	F 10 ESY	F 10 ESY	F 10 ESY	F 10 ESY	F 10 ESY	F 10 ESY	F 10 ESY	F 10 ESY
TUE				F 20 HRD	F 20 HRD	H 20 HRD	H 30 HRD	H 20 HRD	H 20 HRD	H 30 HRD	H 30 HRD	F 30 HRD	U 60 HRD	U 50 HRD	TRK
WED	GYM	GYM	GYM	GYM	GYM	F 20 MED	F 20 HRD	F 20 HRD	F 40 HRD	F 50 HRD	F 55 HRD	F 60 HRD	U 20 ITV	F 20 ITV	U 60 HRD
THU			F 10 ITV	F 10 ITV	F 10 ITV	F 15 ITV	F 15 ITV	F 15 ITV	F 15 ITV	F 20 ITV	F 20 ITV	H 40 HRD	U 40 HRD	U 20 ESY
FRI		F 15 MED	F 30 MED	U 30 MED	U 40 MED	U 40 HRD								F 10 ESY	RAC
SAT	GYM	GYM	GYM	GYM	GYM	GYM	U 40 HRD	U 50 HRD	F 55 HRD	U 60 HRD	F 65 HRD	U 70 ESY	F 20 MED	RAC	F 10 MED
	1	2	3	4	5	6	7	8	9	10	11	12	13	14	15
	\multicolumn{15}{c	}{WEEKS}

H–*Hilly*, U–*Undulating*, F–*Flat*, RAC–*Race*, ITV–*Interval*, ESY–*Easy Pace*
MED–*Medium Pace*, HRD–*Fast Pace*, TRK–*Track*

31

KING OF SPORTS

GEAR CHART FOR 27 INCH WHEELS

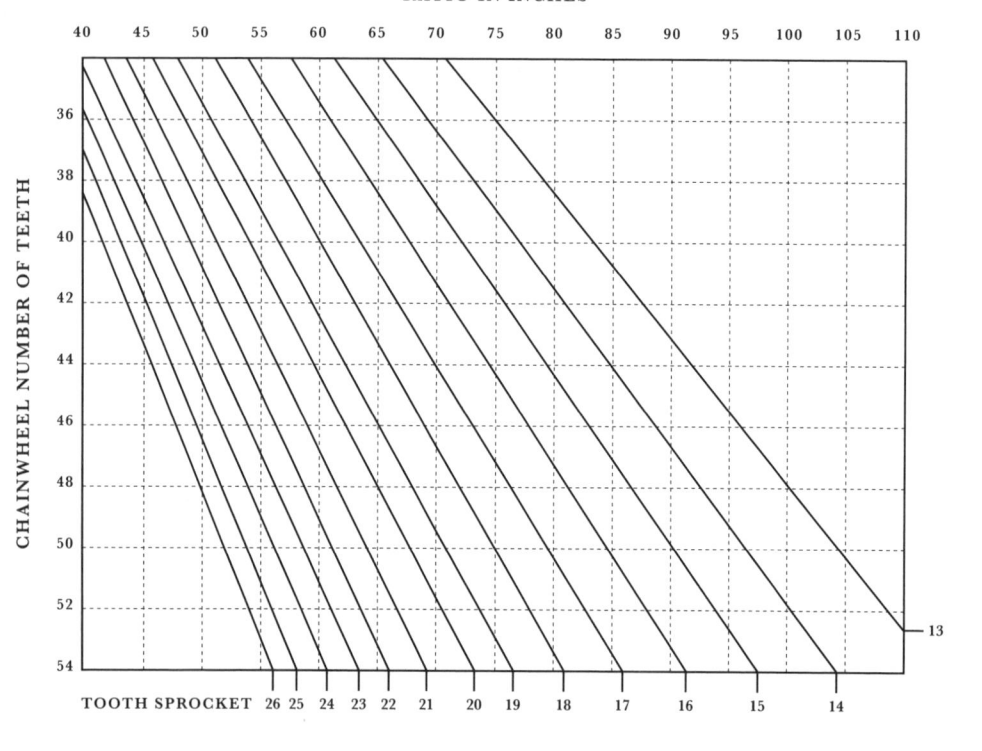

TRAINING

TRAINING TECHNIQUE

With the stamina building miles behind you in your mileage bank, you can start to race without fear of an overdraft.

Once racing has begun your performance must be an indication of your form. After three or four races, if you are improving, leave well alone; if not, use a different routine for at least a month.

One early season after long but steady training runs, I was riding poorly in races and I tried desperately to find a solution. I felt I lacked speed, so I spent the next three weeks doing only 30 mile rides three times a week, absolutely flat out. My next big event I was dropped on the flat.

The Tour of Britain was looming. I was really worried and considered whether I should let a fitter man take my place. I decided to give myself three more weeks. I started doing 60 miles fast, twice a week plus my 20 miles to and from work on the other days. Soon I won two races and all was well.

See how I switched about my training schedule until my form came. On the continent, perhaps, a good coach would do this for you. Over here you have to learn to know yourself.

Keep your diary up to date, noting distance and hardness of your training and racing runs, your weight and pulse rate. It is no use saying: 'I rode well at the end of last season', if you have kept no record of your training programme, which led to this improvement. You will consequently start the new season as unenlightened as you did the one before.

Track racing is invaluable to the road man—to sharpen reactions and increase speed. If you race more than once per week, then cut out some of your training runs.

I personally train hard, but if I blow up in the last ten miles I know that I have been either too far or too fast. I often have to train on my own. When I do, I time myself over each 5 mile stretch using a convenient landmark—a pub, a barn or a tree. I also time myself up a long climb. Sometimes I vary my technique to see if I climb any better. For instance, out of the saddle most of the way, in and out of the saddle, sitting down all the way, sitting well back, sitting forward. This technique of varying your position and gearing can be used on measured, flat and small circuits to gather information on your most efficient and speedy combinations. Often your most natural and comfortable position will be your most efficient.

KING OF SPORTS

The new low friction speedometers are ideal for technique assessment when training. When you have obtained the position you think is right for you and you are riding well, make a careful note of it and stick to it. On the other hand, if you are uncomfortable or not riding well, vary it. My arms were soon tired in spite of training, and I kept raising my handlebar extension, thinking this would take the weight off them. Then I read of a track man who had a very low handlebar position because of his strong back. I lowered mine and I have been alright since.

Listen carefully to advice on your riding, but if you are already improving or you do not take to the change easily, reject it. I am sure if Anquetil had raced as a youth in England many well-meaning advisers would have told him that he would never get to the top unless he lowered his saddle and pushed his heel down.

Good coaches and trainers in this country are few and far between. If you hear of a good one try to visit them to discuss any problems and to obtain advice. If you have any internationals living in your county, try to arrange a visit, and see if they can help you in any way.

Do not spend too much effort and concentration flicking the pedal over the top dead centre of its rotation and clawing it round the bottom (ankling, it is called) unless you do it naturally. Concentrate on a straight pull up and push down, letting your feet get a natural stroking action in between. Ask your friends to watch that no jerky action appears.

Sometimes during training leave your toe straps slack and see if you can keep your foot on the pedal, even when pulling up. If you look at the picture of many famous riders you will note their toes point down on the upward part of the revolution. This I take to mean that the shoe plate is doing most of the work and not the strap.

Use a slightly smaller gear when training on the flat, than you would for racing. As a new rider, start with 66 ins. in January and work up to 74 ins. by April.

If you use a single gear for training either for economy or ease of maintenance, it should be a free wheel. A free wheel gives a better action because it does not rely on the rear wheel to drive the pedals over top and bottom dead centres. Use gears as soon as possible.

To practise regularly an efficient style and a smooth pedalling action is of vital importance to all riders, and especially to those who have developed a fault. For example: one arm pulling more than the other; one foot either grabbing or being lazy; throwing one knee out; tending to change up when the pace is fast; not lifting the pedal by using the shoe plate; not breathing deeply and so on.

TRAINING

To rid yourself of these errors, go out regularly, sometimes with a watchful trainer or friend, and at a steady pace concentrate on eliminating the fault. As you improve, begin to increase your speed.

I feel that speed and more speed is needed by our riders if we are to do well in international competition. Once you have got the early season background of stamina building miles, try and improve your speed by means of short fast training runs, riding behind a moped for a couple of hours, interval training or, best of all, a short evening road race and/or a track meeting once a week.

Don't forget that the difference between the professional and the amateur is not only that the professional can do more miles in training and racing but that he can get more rest. This balance between effort and rest is very important. When you find that even with extra miles your stamina is still lacking, cut down your miles and rest more.

Always give good clear hand signals and be extra polite to other road users, but do not be bullied or put on ; stick up for your rights.

There is no straight and narrow path trodden by every champion, and those who seek a champion's schedule to follow will rarely become champions themselves. Everyone has to find his individual path and will find it only by experiment, trial and error. Just as Van Looy chooses big gears and Charley Caul small; Charley needs little training and Van Looy a lot, you may need to vary your approach from what I have suggested. What I have done is give you a lead.

In the novel, 'Treasure Island', there are many paths from the coast but only one leads to the treasure, and even when starting on the correct one there are many hazards and diversions. I consider I should have saved you trying a hundred paths to nowhere and set you in the right direction, but the rest is up to you. Gone are the days of the all-brawn-and-no-brain athlete. Listen to all the advice and guidance you can, sift it very carefully, then see if you can adapt it to suit yourself.

Some people are born with natural gifts or soon find a training schedule to suit them and they seem to soar to the top. Others have to fight every inch of the way. I find that usually once the fighter makes the grade he is far harder to dislodge and remains at the top longer. Consider for instance the number of people who have become champions after polio and other such crippling setbacks. Many of these people actually start below average, yet the willpower and guts that were used to make them equal are enough to carry them right through to victory.

I can usually tell those who will do well—the ones who are keen usually do too much rather than too little. They are not put off by setbacks but look for the reason for failure, rather than for excuses to tell others.

The path to success is there for everyone, but only those with courage will continue alone in the dark, only those with intelligence will choose the correct turn at the crossroads, and only those with stamina, when the going is hard, will arrive at the summit.

When you have made the grade in this country and you are under 22 years old, especially if you are fast, you must go and live on the continent if you wish to make cycle racing your career.

What is the reward, and is it worth it? To have an object in life is to live. No humdrum routine for the would-be top individual. For the ambition to become a top athlete and to that end to develop the body and the mind is, in my opinion, far superior to becoming a top business executive suffering from the many ailments that are often compatible with overwork of the mind and neglect of the body.

The essential clean living, correct eating and exercising required to get to the top gives a man the appreciation of the true values of life, for few true athletes are concerned with keeping up with the Jones's.

Then, of course, there is the fame and the glory, secondary, I believe, to the attributes mentioned before, but nevertheless worthwhile. When a champion speaks many will listen and youth will often follow; and a good, clear-thinking champion can put forward ideas and ideals that would be neither heeded nor heard of from a lesser man.

Peter Ward racing against Alan Jackson in the National Championships 1956.

CHAPTER 2

EXERCISES

These routines relax the muscles and exercise the lungs, helping to alleviate tension. Do the exercises in front of an open window or in a well-ventilated room. Should any of the exercises tend to strain, do as much as is reasonable and work up your standard as you improve.

I advise you to read some books on Yoga, especially Hatha Yoga. You will discover much that will benefit you as a cyclist, and it will lead you to a fuller life. Do the yoga exercises if you are tired or late and haven't time to do the others.

MORNING AND EVENING EXERCISES

1 Relax, feet together and arms down by your sides. Breathe in slowly, raising your arms forward and up. Raise yourself onto your toes and stretch to reach the ceiling. Hold for five seconds then slowly and completely exhale and relax. Repeat six times. (See Fig. 5).

2

Stand with your feet apart and touch your toes with the opposite hand. Fling your other hand back and up with eyes following. Repeat twelve times. (See Fig. 6).

3

Lie on your tummy with elbows out and hands under your shoulders; straighten the elbows, keeping body straight from head to toe. Repeat as many times as possible, up to twenty-five times maximum, without your chest or tummy touching the floor in between. (See Fig. 7).

4

Hook toes under something that will keep the legs flat along the ground. With hands behind your head and back straight lift your head off the floor and try to touch your knees. Slowly lower and repeat ten times. (See Fig. 8).

EXERCISES

Exercise 1
Deep breathing

Exercise 2
Touching toes with alternate hands

Exercise 3
Press ups

Exercise 4
Abdominal raise

YOGA EXERCISES

1 **Plough posture:** Lie flat on your back, lift your legs up over your head until your toes touch the floor, hold this position for thirty seconds and slowly lower. Repeat twice.

2 **Bow posture:** Lie on your front, bend legs and reach hands behind and grasp ankles. Hold for thirty seconds. Repeat twice.

3 **Sawangasana:** Lie on your back, lift your feet up and, pressing your hands into the small of your back, straighten your back from shoulder to toes, and reach for the ceiling. Carry out once for twenty seconds.

4 Stretch hands above head and stretch the whole body from toes to fingers towards the ceiling.

These exercises should be done at least once a day, all year-round, if possible.

EXERCISES

Yoga Exercise 1
The plough

Yoga Exercise 2
The bow

Yoga Exercise 3
Shoulder stand

Yoga Exercise 4
Standing stretch

KING OF SPORTS
WEIGHT TRAINING

I believe in what Cerutty advises, that a good weightlifter, like a good boxer, trains not only for strength but also to keep his weight down.

The body builder trains to put on body bulk and in training does a lot of repetition with medium weights. The weightlifter uses heavy weights with few repetitions. The cyclist, like the weightlifter, wants strength without bulk. Also, the cyclist should concentrate on the muscles he uses when cycling and not build up bulk and weight strengthening muscles which are not in demand.

For instance, doing squats whilst sitting on the heels exercises a far greater range of muscle capacity than the cyclist uses. Neither does the cyclist fully bend or, as a rule, fully straighten his arms when riding. The morning and evening exercises will keep your other muscles supple and fit.

Start and finish your routine with the Bow and Plough Yoga poses to loosen up. Precede each exercise with four repetitions at two-thirds maximum, two repetitions at three-quarters maximum weight, then one final lift at the maximum weight you can lift. Begin gradually – it is very easy to strain yourself lifting heavy weights, so take two or three months to build yourself up. Relax and breathe deeply before doing another set at the maximum weight you can manage.

1 **To strengthen arms, shoulders and back.** Bend over curling: with legs apart and straight, stand about one foot away from the bar. Bend at the waist and grip the bar, hands one foot apart, keeping your back straight and horizontal. Breathe in deeply then lift the bar two feet off the floor before slowly lowering.

2 **To strengthen stomach and legs.** Put on weighted boots. Place chair back approximately two feet and six inches away. Grip back of the chair and lift alternate feet to a height of one foot and slowly lower, using a pedalling action.

3 **To strengthen buttocks and legs.** With two solidly mounted vertical poles across which the bar can be placed and fastened onto two sleeves. Two stops hold the bar at the correct height. Lie on the floor on a wedge-shaped block, if possible, with your waist under the bar. Place the balls of your feet under the bar six inches apart. Breathe in, then lift before slowly lowering. If you have no apparatus, do short squats. Future champions, I believe, will concentrate on weight training all year-round.

EXERCISES

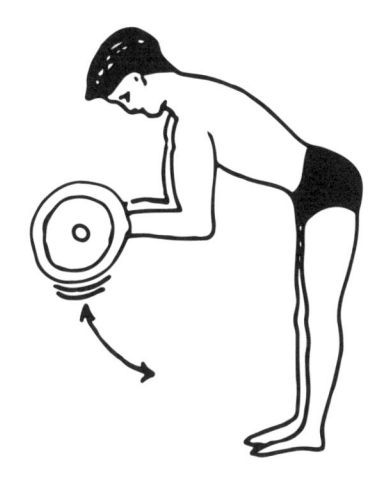

Weight Training 1
Bent over curling

Weight Training 2
Weighted boots

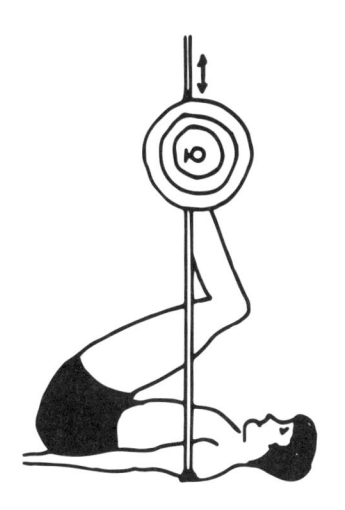

Weight Training 3
Leg press ups

BREATHING

To breathe correctly is of great importance. Treble World Champion Rik Van Steinberghen has stated he considered correct breathing one of the most important attributes of an aspiring cycling champion.

Over 75% of the energy for the muscles comes from oxygen intake so be constantly thoughtful of breathing when training and racing.

Extra lung capacity and a strong diaphragm come from regular breathing exercises. Practice as often as possible when walking, sitting or riding steadily.

When all the air is expelled from the lungs, start to breathe in, filling the lower part of the lungs first. Feel the diaphragm in the stomach hinge down like a large plate drawing the air in. Gradually fill up, finishing with the upper chest. Hold—then with control—breathe out, emptying the stomach first, consciously using the diaphragm, and finishing with the upper chest.

Start by breathing in for four seconds, hold four seconds and out in three seconds. Gradually build up 6—6—5, 8—8—6 and so on, taking care not to strain.

When racing or training fast you usually have to gulp in the air and expel without holding, to stop going into oxygen debt, but whenever the pace eases, breathe deeply without retaining.

CHAPTER 3

MASSAGE

This, I believe, is one of those factors which can be an asset. The professional masseur or masseuse is, of course, the best choice, but if they are the type who are more familiar with footballers, you will have to explain you are a cyclist. Your muscles are used to smooth rhythmic action and, therefore, need more gentle handling. A good practitioner can often feel how fit you are and whether you are over or under training.

If you prefer to massage yourself through lack of money, time, or facilities, here are some helpful hints:

1 Always massage towards the heart.
2 Always use a massaging medium that rubs on easily and comfortably.
3 Concentrate on the arms and legs and, if possible, get someone to do your back and buttocks.
4 If your legs are covered by thick hair, shave them. This makes them easier to massage and keeps them cleaner in races.

I believe it is more important to massage the night before a race than in changing rooms, so that your muscles are more relaxed when getting into bed and have a chance to soak up all the energy and heal any slight damage done in training, or daily routine, during the night's rest. Massage yourself after a training run before going to bed and your muscles will recuperate more quickly.

Relax each group of muscles before you start on them as much as possible. For example, if you are to massage the calf and back of the thigh, bend the knee and, for massaging the front of the thigh, straighten the knee. Grip the muscles with both hands one above the other, pull away from the bone, and roll the muscle from side to side, moving gradually up the muscle all the time. Do this two or three times until the muscles are really loose and then rub on the embrocation with a brisk half slap, half rubbing action, slightly cupping your hands to form an air cushion. Move the hands in a circle, one hand following the other. Do not be too gentle, yet do not hurt yourself by being overzealous. This method can be applied to all the limbs. Complete each section of the limb separately and completely before moving on to the next.

Weather proofing for the bare limbs should be applied in the changing room before the event. In cold weather, something warming – capsucim capsolin or wintergreen compound should be used. In wet weather, something proofing like olive oil. In wet and cold weather a mixture of both on legs, arms, back, buttocks and stomach should be applied.

When training, early in the year, carry a tin of wintergreen. If you feel cold, you can rub the ointment on to warm the affected area.

Once or twice a week have a refreshing salt bath. Use one and a half pounds of commercial Epsom salts (use no soap). Soak for about thirty minutes.

Should you have a fall and twist a limb causing pain and swelling, which does not go down after a day or two, visit a qualified osteopath. An osteopath cured my painful knee which, in spite of visits to doctors and masseurs, gave me trouble for several months.

Never accept one man's council, unless your injury is improving under his care.

CHAPTER 4

DIET

When diet is mentioned, many people retort 'Well, look at such a local champion who lives on fish and chips', or, 'I couldn't live on lettuce'. To their remarks I would reply that the local champion would probably be a national champion if he ate correctly, and that a sensible diet can be made most interesting and varied.

Most people in this country eat far too much and most of us could live quite comfortably on half our present food intake. With our present high standard of living we do not know the meaning of real hunger and the majority of us could comfortably fast for two days without detriment to health.

There is a very important, but often unrecognised difference between hunger and appetite. Hunger is a definite need for the body, but appetite is the habit pattern of the mind tending to promote eating, drinking and smoking to excess. People who let their appetites get the better of them suffer from thrombosis and alcoholism in extreme cases.

Athletes realise the dangers of cigarettes and alcohol, but many do not worry about eating too much. They believe they need a lot more food because they use more calories than a non-athlete but they do not take into account the fact that the latter eats far more than he requires. How often do you feel hungry the moment someone says he is going for a bar of chocolate? You would probably ask him to get one for you also. Had this same fellow said he was going for a slice of bread, your appetite would not have been whetted unless you had been really hungry.

For a cyclist it is nearly as bad to be overweight as underweight, as every pound of fat carried uphill retards the smooth circulation of the blood and hampers fitness. Of course, if you are really under-weight then you will lose strength so be careful not to be too fastidious. During a Tour of Britain, I weighed 11 st. 7 lbs. on average, so I like my weight to be about 11 st. 9 lbs.

My best guide is a pair of accurate bathroom scales – well worth the expense. I note my weight for my best performance and eat accordingly. When I finish racing each year, I still keep at my racing weight by cutting down on my food intake. I used to sweat and struggle during the early season to get my weight down but now I start at racing weight and save myself a lot of wasted effort.

It is a little difficult at first because your stomach and appetite get accustomed to a certain intake of food and, although you have cut down on the energy output, they refuse to be content with less food. A week or so of care and control will soon get your body accustomed to the new and lower food intake. The rest is easy. It is not the muscles turning into fat that makes the ex-athlete into a podgy mess, (muscle bound?), it is through his food intake remaining at its previous level.

If you are a little overweight, cut down on potatoes, bread and other starchy or fatty foods. If you are very overweight, live for a while on plenty of fresh fruit and vegetables (not potatoes). Alcohol, strong tea and coffee impair the efficiency of the kidneys. These vital organs help the body to rid itself of a great deal of waste matter from the blood. Rheumatism, lumbago etc., are caused by overloaded kidneys passing dirty blood back into the system. The blood has to get rid of the waste matter somehow and so it deposits it in the joints and similar places. It isn't 'Joe's Patent Salts' that will give you permanent relief but eating and drinking correctly.

Do not get the idea that all foods that are good for you are expensive, for this is not the case. Fatless beef is as good as steak, ham shank as good as best-ham. Cod fish has a very high protein content. Here is a list of nutritious foods:

Fresh raw	Treacle
Fruit & Vegetable Juices	Eggs
Fresh Fish	Molasses
Fruit	Milk (skimmed)
Fatless fresh meat	Wholemeal bread
Vegetables	Cheese
Brewers' Yeast	Demerara sugar
Honey	Gelatine
Malt	Yoghurt

DIET

Over 70% of the body's daily intake of food should be cleansing food, such as fruit and vegetables. These two should make up the major part of any meal. They provide the body with its main source of vitamins, trace elements and minerals, besides keeping the digestive system clean and efficient.

A juicer (better than a liquidiser) is an excellent investment for good health. The raw juices of fresh fruit and vegetables (especially carrots) are of great nutritional value.

Avoid over-cooked food, especially meat and vegetables. Use cookers that help to preserve the vitamins. Try to make your meals as varied as possible. Get away from the two veg. idea with a cooked meal and have at least three or four. Salads offer endless variety. I am always experimenting. Here is an idea of the fruit and vegetables which can be used. Raw fruit and vegetables ensure the goodness is preserved.

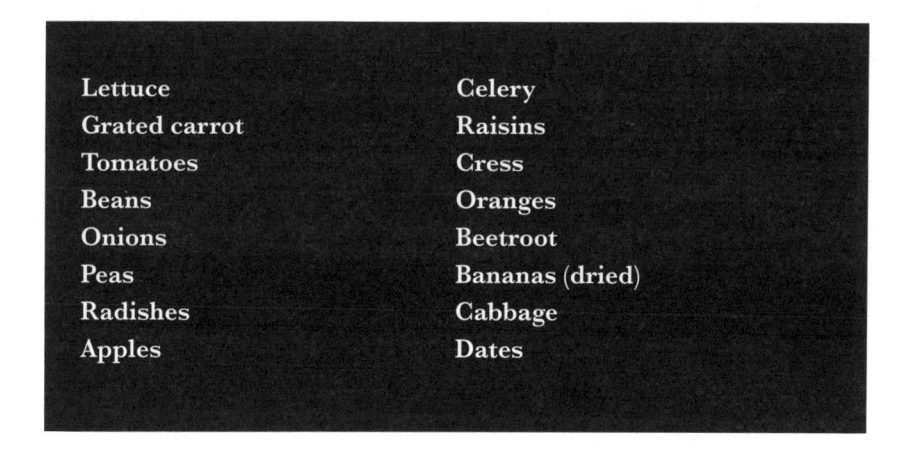

Lettuce	Celery
Grated carrot	Raisins
Tomatoes	Cress
Beans	Oranges
Onions	Beetroot
Peas	Bananas (dried)
Radishes	Cabbage
Apples	Dates

Cheese helps to give bulk to a salad and yoghurt makes an excellent salad dressing. Try to avoid using too much sauce or you will spoil the natural flavour of the food and make everything taste the same.

Here is my typical daily menu during the racing season:

KING OF SPORTS

Before breakfast, gargle and wash out the mouth with lukewarm water. Then slowly drink a glassful of the same.

BREAKFAST

Drink of hot fruit juice.
Lightly boiled prunes.
Porridge (better uncooked)
Grilled lean bacon and tomatoes
Treacle and wholemeal bread (better still, use molasses).

MID-MORNING

Drink of de-caffeinated coffee, or hot health drink.

LUNCH

Fruit drink
Vegetable soup
Roasted (without fat) jacketed potatoes, lightly cooked cabbage, carrots, beans, spinach and fish.

MID-AFTERNOON

Drink of fruit juice.

DINNER

Drink of carrot juice
Lettuce, apple, cress, dates grated carrots and beef
Plums and custard
Whole meal bread and honey.

Half an hour before going to bed have a cup of a hot beverage.
After cleaning the teeth drink a glass of water, preferably warm.

DIET

The digestive system, like the rest of the body, needs not only to rest but time to clean itself out and prepare for the next meal. It takes at least four hours to complete this, so keep your meals well-spaced. Do not eat anything during the two hours before retiring at night so that your stomach can relax and recuperate with the rest of the body while you sleep.

Always remember to chew your food well. This is important and the benefits are well worth the trouble. The stomach's digestive organs will only efficiently utilise starches that are impregnated with mouth juices.

Another advantage is that chewing correctly teaches you to enjoy your food more. Taste is one of our most precious pleasures and one which most of us forget about and neglect. When you chew well you get the maximum taste and maximum goodness out of every morsel. As you chew, think how tasty your food is and how much good it will do you. Your meals will last longer and you will feel fuller and more satisfied with less food.

I believe that an occasional fast does one a world of good. To fast for a complete 24 or 48 hours is not as difficult as you may think, and it gives the digestive system a chance to clear itself of poisons that accumulate over a period of time and also to repair and rest itself. Fasting is particularly beneficial if you get a cold, stomach trouble, boils etc. Many of these ailments are caused because of germs and poisons in the system. Most medicines are only suppressive and only make you feel better temporarily and leave the ailment present. Fasting frees the system from its everyday work and gives it a chance to come to grips with the ailment and to rid the system of it.

Drink at least 5 pints of liquid a day. Always drink slowly. I believe that the drink of water night and morning helps to clean the system. Drink either half an hour before a meal or one and a half hours after, do not wash your meal down.

Be careful about the foods you eat. A racing car would not run very efficiently on pool or low-grade petrol and similarly your body will work at its best only if supplied with correct and good food. I advise you to keep off fatty and fried foods as they are difficult to digest, give little, if any, nourishment, and convert easily into body fat. Avoid minced meat, meat pies, sausages, corned beef, stewed steak and fish cakes, as you cannot see if these foods are pure and fresh. Many of them consist of gristle, fat and meat all mixed together. It is obvious that a butcher will not put a pound of good fresh meat into sausages, and then sell them for half the price the meat would have brought.

White bread, white flour, white sugar, white rice, jacketless potatoes, peeled carrots and apples, the centre leaves of lettuce and cabbage have all had the best parts removed, and eating them is nearly a waste of time. To eat these foods is treating your body like a dustbin, and like a dustbin your body will tend to become germ ridden. Beware of processed, preserved and spiced foods; crops that have been chemically sprayed, and animals fed unnaturally. Colds and catarrh are sometimes proof of a poor diet.

Why say kill the fly? If there was no refuse about there would be fewer flies. Why do doctors say, kill the germ? If there's no waste matter in the body the germs have little to live on. I know several people who have been cured of various 'incurable' diseases by fasting and then living for several months on fresh fruit and vegetables. But do not expect miracles: it takes several months to feel the benefits of a correct diet.

I am surprised that modern physical training instructors do not include diet in their curriculum. To educate our overfed youngsters in this matter would give them more benefit now and in later life than hours of physical exercises.

Get into the habit of going to the toilet at the same time every day; try to go even if you don't feel you are ready. Ensure you go every day, if you miss a day, then take a mild herbal laxative. Should you not return after a couple of days to normal then see your doctor.

Do not be over fastidious; your body will get more nourishment out of food you enjoy than by eating something you dislike. To worry about the food you eat will prevent it being utilized properly.

If you suffer from any illness and your doctor isn't helping you, see a qualified naturopath.

Follow the advice in this chapter, whether racing or not, and live a healthier life.

CHAPTER 5
TRAINING CLOTHES

I begin training at the start of the season when the weather is coldest. Warmth is the main consideration, comfort the next, and finally your appearance.

A cyclist needs to wrap up more than most athletes, because his speed causes the wind to blow away his body heat.

Next to the skin wear a long wool vest and a pair of track suit bottoms or long heavy under-pants (if the bottoms chafe, wear a pair of women's long tights underneath). Never wear brief-type underpants. Apart from wearing out quickly they always tend to crease and become rope-like between the legs. The best type are like shorts with fitting legs.

Over the vest wear either a thick shirt or medium-weight sweater. These two garments should keep most of the sweat confined to them. They should be changed when you stop for lunch on long runs.

On top of this, wear a thicker (preferably zipped) sweater and, finally, a thick windproof (extra-long bodied and sleeved) loose jacket. This jacket must not be waterproof as a waterproof jacket does not breath and causes unnecessary sweating. Extra ventilation holes controlled by zips are a good idea.

Over the tracksuit-bottom wear a pair of tapered or ordinary windproof trousers coming well down round the ankle when the knee is bent. A broad elastic round the foot and stitched creases keep them taut and smart. Keep both pairs of trousers up with a pair of braces and make sure that you have nothing tight round your middle to avoid cramping your breathing and making yourself sweat by stopping air circulation.

On the feet wear a pair of roomy shoes, a pair of thick and thin socks. When it is very cold, and only if you have plenty of room in your shoes, wrap your feet in brown paper in between your socks and shoes. If you can afford them, sheepskin lined shoes are ideal.

On the hands, wear a pair of sheepskin gloves and in your musette carry a pair of light leather gloves to change into should your hands get overheated. Remember, the feet and hands will only keep warm if the wrists, ankles, legs and arms are warm.

Some cyclists suffer from conjunctivitis if the eyes are not protected against the dust and dirt. A pair of lightly tinted goggles with a one-piece curved visor, or night driving glasses are ideal for keeping the cold wind and rain out of your eyes. This helps a great deal psychologically and one is far more cheerful when the sensitive eyes are shaded from the elements.

For the rainy weather: a cape with air circulating netting inside; a cap with a good peak and, in winter, a pair of spats are a help. I have always thought a cape a wind catching and cumbersome waterproof. On training runs I carry a racing-type waterproof jacket, well-ventilated and with air-circulating mesh on the shoulders. I also use over-trousers that cover only the front of the legs and feet.

As the weather improves, discard the large jacket for a tracksuit top. Always try to make sure that upper-body outer clothes can be opened from the neck to welt. By opening them, you can keep your body temperature consistent.

Round your legs wear trousers that fit closely but comfortably, and which preferably finish at the knee (unless specially tailored) with the Richelieu type of stocking. Jeans carefully tucked into long stockings are quite smart. If you wear ankle length trousers, wear white socks if possible. It is essential that the legs give a clean streamlined appearance. This, I believe, makes you feel faster, reduces wind resistance and allows you to see your action more clearly. The knees are the most important part of a cyclist and must never be allowed to feel cold.

In hot weather, shorts with a double seat, wool shirt and white ankle socks keep the rider cool. Beware of the weather going cool in the late evenings.

Next, my delightfully named friend and trusted companion, the 'Musette', crudely called butty, bonk, or food bag by many English riders. It's had a hard time gaining recognition in a country where the saddle bag's reigned supreme, of which many riders are now using badly designed types.

The correct shape is similar to that of a school satchel. I always make my own. The strap should be broad (about three inches wide) and have non-creasing lining to keep flat. Material for the body ought to be tough and waterproof. It should have sides of about three inches and be large enough for carrying all the winter necessities you need for a long run, without too much crushing causing it to become out of shape. 1 ft. 3 ins. x 1 ft, 0 ins. should be the minimum size. Tapes from the bottom corners help to prevent it swinging round when loosely fastened round the waist. When positioned at the bottom of the musette, it should be about 3 inches below the waistline.

No doubt some old timers, and maybe a few young riders, will be saying 'Why not a saddle bag?' In the old days of the Tour de France, when tubulars were heavy,

TRAINING CLOTHES

the riders carried their spares round their necks, which was called 'moving mass'. To see for yourself, put a heavy saddle bag on the bike and climb a hill out of the saddle, then try the same with a musette and see how the bike turns from a heavy unresponsive machine into a lively one.

Do not forget to keep your body warm when off the bike. It is most important to keep the legs and back warm at all times.

RACING CLOTHING

Racing shorts and shoes are the items that should be the most carefully chosen. Expense should not be spared. Do not think, by any means, that I consider the most expensive the best, but leave the cheap items well alone.

Shoes: The leather should be thick on the uppers yet soft and supple. The laces should stretch well down so that they can be adjusted to make the shoe fit throughout its length. Avoid the shoes whose top comes halfway between the toe and the ankle even though they make your feet look smaller. It is no good having a tight toe strap when the feet are loose in the shoes. Choose a pair that finish well up the foot and cannot easily be pulled off when fastened comfortably on the feet When you have selected a pair make sure you undo them well before taking them off, or all your trouble in selecting a close-fitting pair will be wasted. Make sure the soles are made of hard but good leather, the insole must also be leather, and stitched not nailed. Ventilation holes are grand in hot weather, but not so good in cold. If you only use small shoe plates, ensure the instep of the shoe is re-enforced with a spring steel plate.

Socks should also be selected carefully. Two or three pairs will last the season. The best materials are woolen with nylon spliced heel and toe. Nylon and silk are too thin and uncomfortable. Some of the thicker nylon and synthetic material styles are often coarse and tend to chafe the feet. Ensure they have well elasticated tops; nothing looks worse than a rider with his socks collapsed around his ankles.

KING OF SPORTS

Shorts: These should not be made solely of wool – which tends to matt and shrink – or cotton – which usually stretches or goes baggy. My favourites are a wool and rayon mixture. Check the chamois inside: make sure it is very soft; all in one piece and well stitched with no thick overlaps to chafe you. The length of the legs should be half-way down the thigh when seated and, although close fitting, should not feel the least bit tight or restricted. Always use braces and, if you are a cautious type who wishes to retain the fitted elastic top, make sure it is slack and comfortable when you are riding.

Over a mesh vest and braces, in warm weather, comes the racing vest, which can be obtained 'made to measure' quite cheaply. (Although to see some of the 'Bessie Braddocks' leaving changing rooms with pockets filled with food, you wouldn't think it).

The material again, I believe, should be a mixture combining best of both originals. When ordering, give your chest, waist, hip and length (from collar to hem) measurements. A diagram showing dimensions of any design and, if possible, samples of the colours required helps to avoid any disappointments. The length down the back is important, and this should be about 4 inches below the waist when the back is slightly bent. The front pockets should be smaller (about 4 inches deep) and fit high on the chest so that, when full, and if it rains, they will not sag and touch the knees. The top of the pockets should be elasticated so that they will not blow open when riding (most uncomfortable). The best should taper in at the waist and not hang straight from the shoulders looking like mother's parlour curtains. The three rear pockets should be big (about 6 inches deep), strong and, if possible, have a waterproof lining. Ensure they are not so wide as to come round the side of the hips. Again, these should have elasticated openings. For short distance races only, rear pockets are required. Juniors do not need pockets.

Track mitts are difficult to choose. Try on several pairs and choose a pair of soft, washable and well-ventilated ones which, as the saying goes, 'Fit like a glove'.

Racing caps involve the biggest waste of money in clothing. They are expensive and the material they are made of usually shrinks, and the colour runs in the first wash. The peak either frizzles up or flops limply over the eyes at the first gust of wind. They are made in too few sizes. I make my own, but I would like to see some manufacturer eliminating against these setbacks to a good cap.

TRAINING CLOTHES

PROTECTION WHEN RACING IN BAD WEATHER

During early season racing, remember that it is safer to be too warm than too cold. Wear one or two long sleeved sweaters under the racing vest. A large piece of thin polythene front and back under the racing vest keeps the cold wind out and can easily be removed if you get over-heated. Rub some embrocation on chest, stomach, back, arms and feet, using thick wintergreen round the knees and fronts of the legs where they break the wind, and in the small of the back, the stomach and the feet. Wear ordinary leather gloves (or leather and cloth gloves), as woolen ones are too slippery. Use your winter shoes so that you can fit a couple of pairs of socks into them.

Rain is a tricky thing. It can produce a close, sticky atmosphere or it can be bitterly cold, even until June. One of the independent amateur Tours of the Lakes gave me a sharp reminder of this. The race was in June and just before the start it began to rain heavily. Seeing this, I pushed some brown paper under my racing vest, made sure my food was wrapped up in polythene, and off we went. After a fierce start we got a great break of nine riders away from the bunch after only five miles had passed. We soon settled down to a good rhythm and slowly began to gain a few seconds every mile.

At Preston, after 15 miles, we were already 3 minutes up, but by then I was beginning to feel cold and so were several others in the group. We were about to turn into the hills and I encouraged them by saying that the climbing would warm us up, but we remained cold, climbing in the unceasing, icy rain. On the descents some of us were so numbed we could not use our brakes.

At Kendal only four of us were left in the break with an uncatchable lead of 7 minutes, but my teammate, Jackie Brennan, and myself were forced to retire, literally frozen to our machines. Only one of our break, stocky Harry Reynolds, beat the cold and he went on to win the race.

Go out into the rain yourself before a race in your racing clothing and judge what extra clothing you should wear, and whether to put wintergreen on your knees, back and stomach.

Never wear a racing waterproof jacket; you might just as well drag along an aircraft brake parachute.

I use two shapes of waterproofing 1ft. 6ins. x 2ft. square made of thin polythene, one pushed up my front and one up my back inside the racing vest and held in position by my braces. They cannot catch the wind and are easily removed and replaced while riding. Carry them in your pockets if the sky is overcast.

Wear a cap to keep the water running out of your hair into your eyes. Use the glasses I recommend for training, if they are comfortable, to keep the driving rain out of your eyes. If the rain is chilly wear a pair of leather gloves. Should you use a leather saddle, and it chafes in the rain, wear a pair of women's long silk knickers, as I suggested earlier, under your shorts. They enable your backside to slide when your shorts are stuck to your saddle and help you avoid saddle sores.

When you finish a training run or race and you are wet and cold, rub some warm liniment on your back and knees and wrap yourself up extra warm after your bath.

Randy Alsop (left) and Peter Ward (right) heading out for a training ride in 1956.

CHAPTER 6
MECHANICAL EQUIPMENT

If you can afford the initial outlay, then have two machines, one for racing and one for training. This will save you money, but naturally raises the query, 'How can you save when running two bikes?' The answer is: the racing bike should be kept immaculate. To manage this on the cycle which you ride for thousands of miles during training, getting caught in all weathers, would require a major overhaul and some replacements every month. Also, a crash could put your cycle out of commission for several weeks if your frame was badly damaged. If you are going to ride in stage races it is ideal to have your own cycle as a spare.

When you have two cycles make certain the positions on them are exactly the same. Should you be new to cycling, or not sure of your position, start with this one and vary it slightly until you find the one in which you are most comfortable.

First adjust the height of the saddle so that your knee is just, only just, bent with the heel on the pedal and the crank vertically down. Make sure when you do this that you are seated comfortably and centrally in the saddle. Next, with plumb line (or a piece of string with a weight on the end) check the distance of the toe of the saddle behind the centre of the bottom bracket and make it about l in. if you are small, to 2 ins. if you are tall. If you are not sure about the level of the floor, turn the machine through 180o and take the average of the two positions. Check that this alteration, if excessive, has not changed your recently adjusted saddle height. A useful double check for saddle position is to position yourself comfortably on the bicycle, pedal the crank round until it is horizontal and facing forward. Then with the sole of your foot correctly on the pedal, parallel with the crank, a vertical line down from behind the kneecap should pass through the pedal spindle. Set the saddle top horizontal.

The height of the top of the stem is usually about one to two inches below the saddle, measuring horizontally. Any change in the next length is the most expensive and usually means a new stem. Place the elbow on the toe of the saddle and, with the arm running parallel to the top tube, stretch the fingers along the extension. They should be approximately l in. to 3 ins. from touching the handlebars, according to your height and arm length. A high saddle position allows a more streamlined position because the knee does not come up as high and cramp the stomach. A streamlined position is vital and is next only in importance to an efficient and comfortable one.

Nearly all champions present a small frontal area to the wind. Anquetil is a superb illustration of this point.

Be extra careful to put your shoe plates on straight and watch out for cranks or pedal spindles becoming bent. These faults cause many riders knee trouble.

TRAINING CYCLE

It does not matter if your training cycle is a little heavier than your racing bike: use a second hand one; a cheap, slightly heavier one, or your old racing machine. But check that the difference between your two bikes is not excessive. I varied the accessories to obtain the correct position I described earlier.

Wheels: It is surprising how soon a large stock of tubular tyres disappear when doing intensive training, and two or more punctures can cause an unpleasant 'sewing' task when miles away from home. I prefer 27 in. alloy high pressure rims with serrated sides, but even steel rims are quite light these days and also cheap. If you weigh above eleven st. then consider heavier gauge spokes in the rear wheel. I use large, flange alloy hubs with double butted spokes. Quick release hubs are excellent but are not worth the expense if you are hard up.

Tyres: I prefer high pressure tyres to have a pear-shaped section, file tread side and narrow deep line tread round the centre. They should be well matured.

Brakes: These must be centre pull, for efficiency and for self-alignment. A positive quick release and easy fingertip adjustment for tightening the inner cable should be incorporated. Brake blocks must be long, deep treaded and easily fitted into their shoes. These shoes should be easily adjustable in three planes. The ideal brake stirrup is the braized on type. This allows more leverage, easy maintenance and enables easy mudguard removal. The top part of the brake should have long anti-slip levers, with big comfy hoods. Brakes are made, at a reasonable price, that incorporate most of these ideas.

MECHANICAL EQUIPMENT

Gears: Nylon-Plastic, parallelogram rear gears are reasonably efficient and quite cheap. Ensure they cover amply the number of teeth range you require and have positive range control adjustment. Nylon-Plastic front changers are good value and ensure the chain shifter is wide enough to give the chain plenty of clearance when moving across the rear sprockets.

Chainwheel & Cranks: Alloy cotterless cranks five pin and alloy rings are ideal but expensive. If you cannot afford these, choose steel five-pin cranks which fit the same rings used on your racing machine.

Headset: The plastic type.

Extension: Steel if over four inches long, alloy if under four inches.

Handlebars: Alloy 'Maes' shape if you have a long reach, 'Concorde' if you have a short reach. A thick centre for strength and for ease of fitting into the extension. The hooks should be long and bent up and slightly in before fitting. This keeps the tops flat and the elbows in when riding on the bottoms. The width of the bars should be equal to your shoulder width. Use cloth tape for a better grip with a thin strip of sorbo rubber underneath for cushioning. Plastic tape lasts longer but is not very comfortable. I use leather tape I make myself.

Saddle: I have never suffered from saddle soreness or boils on a plastic saddle. Ensure it is well ventilated and has a rough top. There should be ample adjustment to tighten or slacken the top and this adjustment bolt should be easily accessible.

Saddle Pillar: The saddle should be able to be accurately and solidly set at any reasonable inclination and moved forward or backward a minimum of three inches from the centre of the pillar. The locating bolts should be shake-proof and easy to get at, only one spanner should be necessary. Water must not be able to run down the centre of the pillar into the bracket.

Pedals: Some of the very cheap ones are ideal for training on. Make sure they are wide enough to suit the width of your feet, have an oiling hole in the end cap and room for a strap to thread easily through the side plate.

Clips: One piece spring steel with shakeproof nuts (these nuts are not always available). Select a length that puts the ball of the foot over the pedal spindle. Straps: Thick chrome leather, good sharp teeth, extra strong spring and a free roller.

RACING CYCLE

Frame: The frame must be built of 531 double-butted or Kromo tubing throughout. Ensure your main tubes are of sufficient length to enable about 4 ins. of seat pillar to be visible (less if you are still growing). If you prefer your saddle forward, make your seat tube more vertical. Specify the length of top tube so that your extension is under 4 ins. long if possible. Frame square and wheelbase not over 41 ins. I prefer undented chain wheel stays with an oval/round section. The seat stays and forks I prefer round/oval and, unless you are going to race on rough roads, a 1 in. rake is ample. Ends and fork crown should be strong, fitting deeply into the tubes. Make sure the fork head tube is strongly built. Front ends should have a long locating lug at the rear to facilitate easy wheel replacement. I prefer the rear end to be a vertical drop out with a gear boss. Ensure the space across the front and rear ends is the same width as your wheel hubs. This facilitates easy wheel fitting.

In spite of the Italian manufacturers' present contempt for brazed-on fittings, I have rarely seen a good frame that was weakened by them. Clips and screws dotted all over a frame look untidy. Gear bosses, lever bosses, brake and gear cable eyes and rollers, pump pegs are the necessary fittings. Be careful about their positioning, especially the rear brake cable. Ensure that the rear brake cable does not have to be twisted unduly to get round the seat pillar. The best position is 1/8th of the distance round the top tube from the top. Handlebar gear controls with the extra cable required often give a sluggish change. I prefer mine on the head tube because this tube undergoes less stress and the levers are handy. Fit the pump out of the way in front of the seat tube, using the push-on adaptor end fitting.

Wheels: Alloy Road sprint rims, balanced with reinforced section. Deep, strengthened spoke holes. Serrated sides (if possible). Hubs: alloy, large flange, quick release with the lever working across the spindle end. Cones extra hardened and polished, both with wide spanner flats. Locknuts with a narrow bearing surface on the frame sides. Spokes: light, tensile steel double butted – have them tied and soldered.

MECHANICAL EQUIPMENT

Tubulars: 9 ½ ozs. pear section, file tread on the sides, thin deep line tread around the centre, puncture preventative internal strip. Tyre savers are well worth fitting. Ensure your spare tubular has been used, so that it is well stretched and cemented.

Gears: Both levers should be strong and easily tensioned by hand. There ought to be equal and reasonable movement of the lever between each gear. The cable nipple should fit easily into the lever body. The gear cage should, ideally, follow the line of the sprockets equal distance and close to each one. The chain must have ample wrap round each sprocket, so always choose one which easily covers the number of teeth change you require. Chain tension should be easily adjusted without using tools.

The gear must have positive, separate and easily adjustable stops. The ideal method for an efficient change is for the cable to pull the chain up to the large sprockets and the spring to return the chain down the sprockets. A lip should prevent the gear going into the spokes. The chain tension should be adjusted automatically when the chain wheels are changed. The ideal material is nylon-plastic for the gear body and rollers. Cheap parallelogram gears are made with many of the points mentioned here and they are reasonably efficient.

Chainwheel and Cranks: Alloy, five pin with solid square fitting to the spindle. Many types work loose, so try to ensure a good locking device is incorporated. Stops should be fitted to prevent a derailed chain getting jammed behind the crank or chain-stay. Make sure they accommodate a large variation in chain-ring sizes.

Block: An ideal design is one in which sprockets and the block body are all easily removable —several times if necessary. Three pawls are to be preferred, and it should be reasonably water-proof.

Continentals often overlap gears to get the gears they prefer and to minimise use of the chainrings. What a waste! This is how I group my gears to gain the advantages above and also to obtain minimum overlap. Rings 38—54, sprockets (ensure that the rear gear will accommodate the number of teeth change). Place spacers between the rings and the gear side bottom bracket cup if the chain, when on the small sprocket and small ring, catches on the large ring. Triple rings and six blocks give even more scope and more trouble.

Pedals: If you have narrow feet then the platform type of pedal is the best design (only narrow ones seem to be made). I can see neither sense nor reason in the saw tooth narrow edged pedals that flood the market. I would like to see a wide platform pedal with specially designed shoe plate to fit. In the meantime, choose a light pair with alloy shell and hardened steel ball bearing housings. Ride new shoes without plates on first, so that the pedal mark on the sole will show where to fix the plate.

Most other equipment can be selected as I advised for the training cycle. When you cannot afford the initial outlay for two cycles, if possible, have a pair of sprint wheels and use them only for racing. Give your cycle a thorough check at least once every two months and clean it before every race. I won my first race on wired-on tyres, wearing a modified football jersey as a racing vest. Never miss racing because your bike is not one of the best; if it is safe and clean, you are fine.

CARE FOR YOUR RACING MACHINE

To start the new season all bearing surfaces should be cleaned and all balls and cones replaced on any machine used the previous season. Not all manufacturers grease bearings, a fault they should remedy, so check them yourself on a new bike. Use a light grease and check that every locknut is rock tight against its cone when you re-assemble.

Change all inner and outer brake and gear cables. Ensure the inner cables are coated with a thin layer of grease and they slide easily along the outer cover.

Change toe straps, handle-bar tape, brake hood rubbers, brake blocks, tyre-savers and anything else that is worn or rusted.

Check your rims for dents, have the wheels trued, remove any spokes that will not adjust easily and replace block and chain. Examine the chain rings and both gear mechanisms for wear and replace if necessary.

Some of the items you have changed might have lasted another dozen events or so, but others may let you down in the very next race. Do not waste them; use them up on your training bike or keep as spares for it.

Go out training on your racing machine at least three times before you race. Have new wheels re-trued and re-check all nuts. If you use the machine only for racing, it should need only one more overhaul to make it last the season. Here are a few tips:

MECHANICAL EQUIPMENT

1. On the rear wheel set up the block side cone first and lock it with a locknut very tightly, then put in your spacing washers and finally your end locknut. This means once your wheel is set up you can fit an extra washer or remove one for gear alignment without disturbing the bearing setting or removing your block. Only leave about 3/16 in. of spindle showing on quick release hubs.

2. Fit a piece of loose cardboard or tin in between the bottom bracket cones so that it contours the bracket shell. This prevents pieces of brazing working loose and dropping down the tubes into the bottom bracket. Another item that is only fitted by a few manufacturers.

3. Wirelock the locking ring on the bottom bracket and it will never work loose.

4. Tie a piece of nylon stocking round the bottom head set bearing. It keeps out all the dust and dirt thrown up through having no mudguard.

5. Tape brake levers to the bars so that if a crash breaks the clip or it works loose the tape will keep the lever in place.

6. Store tubulars for at least 6 months before they are required or ask your dealer to do this for you. I believe that storage hardens the rubber and makes the tyres last longer. I wish that all manufacturers would ensure that all tyres are matured before allowing them to be marketed.

7. When fitting new tubulars to the rim, ensure the rim is clean. Place the tubular on the rim and lightly inflate. Roll the tubular back from the rim, 6 ins. at a time. Lightly brush the rim cement onto the rim, roll the tyre back in position and continue this process right round the rim.

8. Soften your tyres when racing in the wet; to allow more of the tread to come into contact with the road.

9. Avoid riding new tyres in the wet, the shiney hard surface makes them more prone to skidding.

CHAPTER 7

PREPARATION

Do not train hard two days before a race unless you are still in the process of gaining fitness.

Try and get to bed two nights before the event, even a little earlier than usual, giving your muscles time to repair and relax.

Check and clean your machine two evenings before the event so that you have time to replace any faulty item, and you are not up all pre-race night trying to find a nut with a Continental Thread, or something similar. Go out for a trial run on the morning of the day before a race. Find a suitable hill over which to function all the gears and see if you can pull your wheel over.

Check any new fitment with extra thoroughness. Always ride new equipment and new wheels several times and have the wheels re-trued before racing on them.

If you are going to stay overnight near the race, ask the organiser to arrange your accommodation. It saves a lot of tramping around in the late evening. Write and tell your host what food you would prefer, and when, in plenty of time. Most will oblige at little extra cost, if any. It is unfair to expect a harassed landlady to find a couple of steaks at 7 o'clock on a Saturday evening.

Buy all the food you require for the race early the day before. Always make out a list of the articles you need for a race, on a stiff piece of white cardboard, and keep it where you can find it. There are so many things to remember that it is difficult to remember everything. Here is a list of what I take:

Cap, vest, spare sweater, racing vest, shorts, braces, waterproofs for front and back, white socks, cycling shoes, track mitts, ordinary gloves. Extras – racing licence, sunglasses and/or goggles, small sponge, vaseline, embrocation, wintergreen, olive oil, small adjustable spanner, pressure pump, towel and soap, crash helmet.

Keep your eye on all the results you can find every week throughout the season. Remember to note down the winners and runners-up in the type of events in which you are competing.

When you get your programme, browse through it, especially if you are riding away from your area. Mark off the best four or five riders. Make sure you find them in the changing rooms before the race starts and note their colours and numbers so that you can recognise them immediately in the race.

PREPARATION

Meet the rest of your team before race day and discuss your general plans for the race. Make up your mind what your team is capable of. Here is how to do this: if you have one rider finishing often in the first four and the rest of you outside eighth place, then your job is to try for an individual win for your best teammate. When you have a team in which two riders often finish inside the first five, still help these two to try to win individually and keep half an eye on the team race which you may get anyway. Should your team usually finish inside fifteenth and outside sixth, then concentrate on a team win. When you have no man inside the first ten, then ride individually, helping each other if it does not waste too much energy, until one of you manages to get a place in the first five, which would warrant the rest of the team's help.

The best way to win races, is to race with skill. The best way to become fit enough to win races, is to race hard; these two do not usually go together. I therefore suggest you race carefully to win, one week, and ride aggressively, to improve your strength, the next week.

Many of the Continental racing clubs have a discussion during the club night, and the team managers report on how the team rode and on any bad tactics used by his team. The offending rider has the opportunity to explain his action. Should his reason be poor, he is told what he should have done and why. In your club, the riders should discuss each other's riding and report each other's faults so they can be corrected.

During a Tour of Britain our team managers cautioned a rider for the following piece of thoughtless riding –

The stage was 110 miles long, and after 70 miles I had pulled away on my own. Ten miles further on I was caught by a teammate and a Spanish rider.

Shortly after, my fresh teammate attacked and left both the Spaniard and myself behind. After a mile, I also dropped the continental and chased my companion who was a hundred yards or so ahead. Although I shouted for him to wait, and a motorcycle marshal passed on my request, he pedalled on.

At the finish, after the pair of us had time-trialed the last 30 miles, he beat me by half a minute.

Our manager pointed out to us, had my teammate waited for me and the two of us worked together, we would have been faster and finished less fatigued. And even in the unlikely event of him having to pace me to the finish, he would have helped the team and his companion.

Our boss also pointed out to me the folly of attempting long, lone breakaways. He was so right! In the next stage, I was so tired from the previous day's effort that I had to fight to stay with the bunch.

HOW TO CORNER

Practice fast but safe descending while training so that you know what you are capable of. It is not the road conditions, gravelly or slippery though they may be, that cause you to skid. As a rule, it is your bad riding under the conditions. Even when it is wet on a long straight part of a descent you should let your bike fly. Do not descend for a quarter of a mile at 20 m.p.h. and take the corner at 12 m.p.h. to catch up those riders who descended at 30 m.p.h. and took the bend at 8 m.p.h. You will be the unseated rider, for it is the speed on the bend that matters.

200 yards before the bend, if the road is wet, lightly apply your brakes to clean the water off the rims and dry the brake blocks without slowing down. At 150 yards tighten your grip on the lever and check your bike's response. If it is not so good, grip tighter until it does respond, getting ready to slightly release pressure to prevent a skid if your wheel suddenly locks. At 100 yards start slowing rapidly so that you reach your required speed 20 yards before the bend. Should you then see the bend is only shallow, release your brakes and away. If it is steeper than you thought, you have 20 yards to slow down more rapidly. Release your brakes as soon as your bike starts to lean.

When, through bad anticipation, you think you are going too fast, carry on into the bend as normal (this applies under wet or dry conditions), keep your brakes on tight until your machine starts to lean and watch out for wheel lock as above. When you start leaning, clatter the brakes on and off quickly so that no sooner than your wheel locks and begins to skid, they are released again. Remember to lean further and further if necessary. It is surprising how far a machine will lean before it skids from sideways pressure. If you doubt my word, watch the motorcycle races.

It is nearly always the wheel locking that causes the skid. Also, if you do come off it is far less dangerous, for you slide along and your machine takes the first impact; you will only hit the road with a glancing blow. When a wheel locks, the cycle loses steered direction and goes in the centrifugal direction. Should you panic going into a bend and head straight for the roadside you will hit it with far

PREPARATION

greater impact. Of course, if a grass verge or hedge is handy, they make an even softer crash barrier.

When entering a corner, in company, never cut either verge unless forced to and always leave enough room for one rider to flash through either in an emergency or because he descends faster than you. The direction or line you take through a corner matters a great deal and is proportional to the speed at which you take it.

In this country we have to share the road in a race with other vehicles and you should never forget it. This means that you should plan every corner with the thought that something may be coming the other way. My method is to use all the permissible road required that I can see, so I end up round the corner where I can't see as far over on the left hand side of the road as possible. Fig. 16 and 17, illustrate this. If you are unsure follow the same line as one of the best descenders in your race but about 15 yards behind. If he makes a mistake you have time to slow down.

After a race, any crash should be analysed and, if there is a rider who is without doubt guilty of causing other riders to fall, he should be suspended for a fortnight and fined the money to help repair the innocent victims' broken machines.

These careless riders give the sport a bad name especially with the police; they cause a great deal of injury and expense to other competitors, who are blameless. Under the present system, apart from a few curses from fallen riders, they go scot free.

KING OF SPORTS

Bill Bradley, Peter Ward and Eric Wilson at the Lakeland Division Championships 1957.

CHAPTER 8
GOOD SPORTSMANSHIP

1 Good sportsmanship, I believe, is a key attribute of road racing. In my cycling career I have met few incidents of bad behaviour. The main points to watch are:

2 Obey the Highway Code. Upon this I think the future of our sport on the open highway depends. Anyone endangering this present right should be punished.

3 Never attack or overtake when approaching a corner or congested part of the road. You could injure yourself as well as rivals afraid you might break away and therefore follow you.

4 Try not to attack, after a crash or puncture by other riders, and add to any confusion that may have developed (although do not get caught napping even if others are). Your win should be by superiority, not by your opponents' bad luck.

5 Always, verbally and by hand signal, warn riders behind of potholes, mechanical or puncture trouble, vehicles parked on the left, sharp corners, halt signs, etc.

6 Riders on the outside and at the rear of the bunch must give hand signals to indicate any changes in the speed or direction of the bunch, to traffic behind.

7 Never use bad language either to competitors or to other road users. A telling-off for any misdemeanor, without bad language, makes far more of an impression on an offender.

8 Never ride more than two abreast unless you are overtaking. Don't float up and down the outside of the bunch like a lost soul, obstructing the road and making it difficult for other riders to overtake safely.

9 Unless you are defending, keep close to the rider in front and close any gaps you let open through negligence. Don't wait for another rider behind to use his energy to cover your mistakes.

10 Never swerve or brake suddenly. Always be considerate to the riders behind. Riders should not be allowed to change direction after 100 yards to the finish. I am amazed at the number of top professionals who crash. I would have thought their concern for their livelihood would make them more careful and considerate.

11 Stop dead at halt signs and put your foot firmly down. If everyone did this one of our biggest faults would cease. Why does every rider think he will lose time and so get annoyed if a policeman is not there to wave him on. It is time all riders realised that if everyone stops correctly at halt signs, police controlled or not, no one will gain an unfair advantage in bunch or breakaway.

12 Don't use the old trick of trying to break away at the feeding station. It is dangerous and is bad sportsmanship. Everyone would get his food and drink and no helpers would get hurt if the riders slowed down to 5 m.p.h. through the feeding area. But don't be off guard if other riders take advantage.

13 Don't descend faster than you are safely capable of. It is wiser to lose 3 seconds on a corner than three weeks in a hospital. But if you continually get left behind on the descents you must have courage and learn to hold the good riders. It is silly to fight hard, pedalling back ground lost through freewheeling.

RACING PSYCHOLOGY

As Fausto Coppi once said, 'Always remember that the other chap is suffering just as much as you are'. Hard to imagine with Coppi, but it shows he knew a great deal about psychology, one of the most important phases of the sport.

Dick Bartrop from Sheffield, the famous independent, and twice winner of the first stage of the Tour of Britain, once told me the following story— He was in a two-up breakaway with about five miles to the finish with the bunch a long way behind. Dick was feeling shattered, and every time the unknown chap he was partnering went to the front he went so fast he nearly left Richard behind. Realising brains not brawn would be needed to beat this chap, Dick put all his effort into a mighty spurt, and as he overtook his rival he shouted, 'Come on, move it, unless you want us to get caught'. The chap, who had been giving his best, thought it was not good enough. Thoroughly demoralised, his legs went dead and he dropped behind and Dick went on to win.

Sunglasses hiding eyes lined with strain; a cap hiding tousled hair, clean shaved legs and easy style drop many a flustered untidy rider behind because he is convinced the immaculate looking rider cannot be suffering as much as he. A clean, trouble-free cycle inspires confidence.

One of the things your training miles should do is to teach you your most comfortable positions. Use the same positions when racing. Don't go down on the drops for all the race because it feels hard sitting up. Don't climb out of the saddle because some chap is making it look easy – unless you do so in training.

Breathe as deeply as possible all the time and try not to over gear because it feels hard. It is far easier to relax in a lower gear.

Always look over the shoulder of the rider in front. Don't keep your eyes glued to his back wheel. Not only is it bad psychologically and makes you feel like a hanger on, but it is also dangerous and bad tactics, as I shall explain later on.

The temperamental athlete gets rid of his pent-up worries and emotions and is usually a good performer. The people who think they have no worries bottle up their feelings, which can lead to loss of form. If you can't relax, then go to someone who can teach you to relax and you will become a better rider.

Without being 'big headed', allow yourself to feel confident before a race. Tell yourself again and again that you are going to win. During your training build up your confidence. Do not give yourself any reason to say, 'I should have trained this or that way, but I didn't'. Work out your training programme carefully so that you have full confidence in it.

EATING & DRINKING WHEN RACING

Try and have a good meal about two hours before any road race, giving time for the most heavy part of the digestion work to be completed before the race starts. Don't forget that digesting uses up energy. When the race is under 50 miles try to avoid eating anything in the two hours before the race.

Should your race be over seventy miles a light snack or a few sandwiches about half an hour before the start will give you energy in the race.

Fifity miles and under: nothing to eat or drink during the race. Your body has ample reserves to cover this distance. You will waste time and energy eating and digesting. Half a peeled orange to clear your mouth on a hot day.

Sixty miles: Three-quarters full bottle, one sandwich, one packet of glucose tablets (medium) or a handful of sugar lumps.

Eighty miles: One full bottle, three sandwiches, a handful of sultanas, one banana, a handful of sugar lumps, orange (peeled), bar of chocolate.

One hundred miles: Two full bottles, four sandwiches, a handful of sultanas, two bananas, two handfuls of sugar lumps, orange, bar of chocolate.

One hundred and twenty miles: Two full bottles (drinking), one full bottle liquid rice and sultanas, two bananas, eight sandwiches, two handfuls sugar lumps, orange, two bars of chocolate.

GOOD SPORTSMANSHIP

This list is just a guide, many riders can do with less, some need more. When there is a feeding station in the longer races carry less, but enough to see you through if you miss your feed.

Watch what other riders eat and try their ideas whilst training before you include them in your racing diet. I enjoy jam or honey on bread, half slices, with the crust cut off and rolled up like small swiss rolls and wrapped individually like sweets. A diluted honey drink and dried fruit are easily digestible and excellent energy foods.

It was so hot when I rode in the Tour of Britain that we were unable to eat food after the first ten miles because our throats were so parched. I overcame this by taking thin rice pudding, powdered glucose and sultanas mixed in one of my bottles. With anything else I ate, I took a drink of water to enable me to swallow it.

You must discipline yourself and make sure you ration your food and drink to last you the full distance. Eating in a race should be carefully planned. I usually eat heavy food first, Kendal mint, chocolate and sandwiches. Next dates and glucose and finally, near the end, glucose and oranges. Eat slowly, chewing well. Spread your food out to cover the whole race. Descents or steady periods are the best times for eating, but any time you are not actually making an effort at the front will do. A little and often should be your aim.

A well-known rider told me how, due to the excitement of an early break and constant action throughout the race, he forgot to eat. When away on his own with ten miles to go he got hunger knock and said that his pockets were full. Although he ate quickly the damage was done. He finished exhausted, four minutes behind the winner.

If you have done as I have told you and done without drinks on training runs, you will find, with a little discipline, you can make one bottle go a long way.

Early in my racing experience I used to think, 'replace lost sweat as quickly as possible', and drink gallons. Every minute of the race, especially on hot days, my throat was parched, I borrowed from other riders, and on one occasion stopped at a wayside fountain and lost valued time. I have found that discipline is essential where drink is concerned— 'Soft Drinks Anonymous' I have called it and all racing men and women should join if they want to succeed.

You will find that if you do not drink for a reasonable amount of time, you will get a little thirsty, but this thirst stage stays at the same level. However, if you drink, the thirst is momentarily cured, but in a short while it comes back worse than before and so it goes on—a vicious and tormenting circle.

KING OF SPORTS

In a seventy-mile race drink nothing for the first forty miles, then drink one third of your bottle slowly and all at once, preferably at the bottom of a descent and not at the top of a hill where you might be feeling extra thirsty. Drink another one third after fifty miles and the rest at ten miles to go. Do not pick up drinks from spectators unless you have arranged with a friend to hand you a drink to coincide with where you would use your own bottle (to save you carrying the weight).

Should you carry a flask of sherry or very strong coffee, only drink it if you have a chance of winning. With ten miles to go, drink half and at five miles, the remainder. It is just a mild stimulant and can help a little, but it is no use whatsoever if you ordinarily drink alcohol or coffee during the weeks before the race.

During a stage race abroad, one of the England team had saved a bottle for the final twenty miles. The sun was beating down, the roads were dusty, and mirages kept appearing in the hazy distance. One of the Polish riders, with his dry tongue hanging out, begged the British rider for a sip. Reluctantly and indicating only a sip he handed the Pole his bottle. Grabbing the bottle he drank half and then poured the rest over his head, much to the amazement and disgust of the English man.

The next stage was even hotter and the English rider purposely saved another full bottle and with twenty miles to go he rode alongside the offending Pole. Smiling, he made a great show of enjoying half the bottle, watching the Pole's face crease with distress. Then he offered him the rest of the bottle and the Pole gleefully swerved across to take it. As he reached out the English rider upturned the bottle and the agonized Pole watched the precious liquid gurgle out of the bottle and disappear in the dust on the road. This is a story with many morals.

Drugs are a disgrace and a danger to all sports and sportsmen.

Most sports pretend the problem does not exist. Cycling is one of the few sports trying to eliminate this evil.

Records can keep being broken because the mind gives the heart and body ample protection against strain. Technique and hard training strengthen muscle and willpower, but the protection gap stays about the same.

Drugs skilfully administered can partially close this gap and increase performance. Drugs can, unskilfully administered, eliminate the gap and cause immeasurable damage to the body.

An unscrupulous athlete near the top of his sport pays a quack doctor well and draws level with the top man. The top man pays well for drugs and advice and pulls in front again. A vicious and stupid circle.

An unscrupulous 'win at all costs' country can be willing to gamble a youth's future for one gold medal.

A thoughtless youth or hard-up professional hears what drug is being used, obtains some, and guesses the amount, often with drastic consequences.

What do we do? Even things up and allow all athletes free use of drugs, something ordinary people are not allowed to do, and trust no stupid or selfish rider will risk taking a little extra to go a bit faster. This would be ridiculous; we cannot allow them.

Care must be taken to make the ban effective and to protect the individual. This would be done by (a) having unannounced tests at the finish of several classics and a few minor events; (b) under strict supervision, taking two carefully sealed and labeled samples from each of the leading riders. One kept by the organizer or local division for any cross checking, or for the rider to have an independent check; the other to be sent for analysis; (c) riders should not exchange food or drink and team managers should ensure drinks are not tampered with before the start of events.

A rider whether amateur or professional, should be banned for at least six months for the first drug offence. For a second offence they should be banned for life.

RIDING IN THE BUNCH

Assuming that you are not interested in any breakaway, or if all the riders are together, choose a position as much out of the wind as possible, yet not too hemmed in by other riders. Ride relaxed on the top of the handlebars and in a slightly lower gear than when you are in the breakaway or making a special effort. Do your 'bit' at the front when required but make it short and brisk – there are plenty of others to share the work. Try to keep within calling distance of your teammates, if possible, but not too close in case the whole of the team is knocked out of the race in one unfortunate crash, so everyone is on hand to help each other. Keep your eyes open all the time for your main rivals in the bunch making any move, or for a suitable place for you or your team to attack.

KING OF SPORTS

Always keep near the front of the bunch. Remember that the front man is accelerating out of the bend when the last man is still braking fifteen yards from it. By the time the last man is crawling round the corner the first man is 50 yards down the road moving at 25 m.p.h. The further you are from the front the bigger the gap you will have to close.

When you are feeling tired, try and keep in the most sheltered place you can find. Move nearer the front of the bunch on easy stretches so that you can afford to drop back when the going is hard without going off the back of the bunch. Don't make a nuisance of yourself getting in the front echelon or leaving gaps for other riders to close.

When there is a strong cross wind on an exposed piece of road you must make every effort to get in the front echelon. If this is not possible, start another echelon. Do not grovel in the gutter trying to get protection from another rider who is also in the gutter when the wind is coming across from the right. If the second and third echelons keep close to the front echelon, they will be even better sheltered from the wind.

I have seen many a front echelon group pull away from a full bunch just after the start of several classic events because riders behind would not organise themselves. Often a lone rider of experience will swing out into the centre of the road and shout for other riders to join him only to be ignored by the foolish riders in the gutter; he then finds himself blown back down the road. In the Tour-de-France the experienced professionals know how much effort is saved by riding in echelon; I have often seen them form four or five separate lines, each about 10 to 20 yards behind the group in front. Fig. 18 shows this.

In a Continental stage race I was told by the British team manager to go with the first break on the first day. I now realise this was a bad mistake. Every rider in a new country should learn to settle down first, on a stage race, and have as quiet a ride as possible until he knows what he is up against.

Anyway, I did as I was told and after about five miles we got a break of ten away. I was thrilled. I worked like a demon but, looking behind every mile, I noticed that our 300 yards lead never increased. After 20kms, we were caught at the bottom of a climb and I was too shattered to hang on.

During later stages when I settled in and rode quite well, I noticed, to my amazement, that the front of the bunch did bit and bit continually. The speed of the bunch rarely dropped below 25 m.p.h. If you wanted to do well, you tried to join this group at the front of the bunch. I say 'tried' because you literally had to push your way in.

Should you drop further back than twelfth or so, you were back with the main bunch. In England that is the easiest place to be, but on the Continent in the front group the pace is steady and there are no gaps opened. The bunch just behind is constantly changing speed and large gaps keep opening. If you stay there too long you will soon be struggling off the back of the bunch.

This, I believe, is a major reason for the Continentals being faster, for they have to work in the bunch, and to break away from the fast-moving bunch. Staying away takes some doing. Whether there is a breakaway or not, be prepared to do your work to keep the bunch moving at a steady pace. Your effort should be short, as there are enough riders in the bunch to spread the work out. It will make your racing more enjoyable, with no dull, slow patches, and will stop undeserving breaks winning by a ridiculous margin. It will also make for the overall improvement of all British competitors.

Our below-classic-standard and junior races are pathetic for their lack of pace in the bunch. Riders will free-wheel when it is their turn to do a 'bit' at the front instead of moving through. Some riders seem to go to sleep in the middle of the bunch and never see the front except by accident. You hear them in the changing room moaning about how hard they train whilst never doing well in races. The reason is obvious: unless you race hard you will never be good. Australian Handicap road races are ideal for third & junior races.

Don't sit back in the bunch when a breakaway of top riders is disappearing. Get to the front, with some of your team if possible, and help the chase.

RIDING IN THE BREAKAWAY

I mean here a group in which all riders are concerned with staying away from the bunch. 'Out of sight, out of mind' is a good maxim that can be applied to road racing. The bunch tend to go a bit easier once the breakaway group of riders disappears from view, so when your break is this distance clear, slow down your pace gradually to one you feel you can keep going until the finish. Ride as relaxed as possible and use the positions you use when training unless the circumstances are different, i.e. when there is a head wind.

If there are a lot of you in the breakaway, make your period at the front short; on the other hand, if there are only a few, make it long. Remember the advantage you have over the bunch is that you are all pulling together and your speed is constant. A gain of only 5 secs, a mile over 12 miles gives you a minute margin, so keep close together, especially on descents and corners. Do not waste the energy of the other members of the breakaway by accelerating out of the halt signs and steep corners when you are the first rider through. Look round and wait until the group is together before increasing the pace. It is a useless waste of the riders' energy to keep closing the gaps you cause to open. Energy, when used at the front, can be used to keep you out ahead of the bunch. When you are at the back or in the middle, keep the rider in front close and do not let gaps open. These gaps wreck the morale and the speed of the group. Change smoothly and get together quickly after any primes or hold-ups.

When you are a better climber or descender than the rest do not leave them (until you are sure you can make the finish on your own) but ease up and ride with them and encourage them to go a little faster. Eat your food and drink on the way back down the group, not at or near the front when all attention is on the effort you are making. Change gear before you take your turn at the front when a different gear is needed. Do not clang about with your gears at the front at the last minute and slow everyone down. Should the man in front of you be going slow for any reason (mechanical or otherwise) get past him and do not let the speed slacken.

When you get dropped by the breakaway because you find it hard, or because they are going too fast for the distance remaining, do not keep trying to get back with them unless you are near the finish. Relax, push a small gear, breathe deeply and have a little to eat (do not stuff yourself with food) and wait for the bunch to catch you.

When the wind changes and causes you to take shelter on the other side, instruct the front rider, who will not feel the change as much as those sheltered at the back, to also change side. Never ride with your eyes glued on the wheel of the man in front of you. If you do you will not notice obstructions in the road, break-ups in your group or the change of side at the front due to wind change. Always look over his shoulder. Nothing is worse than riding echelon on the left of some forgetful rider who forgets and changes to the left. This can cause some nasty accidents, so keep your wits about you.

When there are six or more riders in a group (especially riding against a wind) and you have just swung off the front, wait for the next rider to swing off and ride close to him back down the group. This enables you to gain protection nearly all the time, and also prevents a large knot of riders getting tangled up at the rear of the group from dropping back too quickly. Figs. 18, 19, 20, and 21 illustrate.

When you are at the front, remember to leave a space for the other riders to shelter (unless you are trying to break away from them). It is no good riding in the left gutter when the wind is blowing from the right or you will have the rest riding on the footpath to gain shelter.

When there is a larger group, have the common sense to make several small echelons so that the riders do not cross the centre half of the road. Nothing looks worse and gives the sport such a bad name as riders from gutter to gutter on a windy day. I think that mobile judges should give a warning to each rider and then, if anyone crosses the white line again, he should be disqualified or in a stage race receive a minute penalty each time he is told.

If the following judges withdrew one careless rider per event, early in the season, I am sure the behaviour of the few thoughtless riders would improve, benefiting the whole sport, other road users and the police.

If a rider in your breakaway (or bunch) is too strong or inexperienced and is going so fast when it is his turn at the front that he keeps splitting the group, then it is a wise move to let him go (especially into a head wind). Better than waiting while he drops you, one at a time, and you are left shattered, without company, and without hope of catching him or of staying away from the bunch.

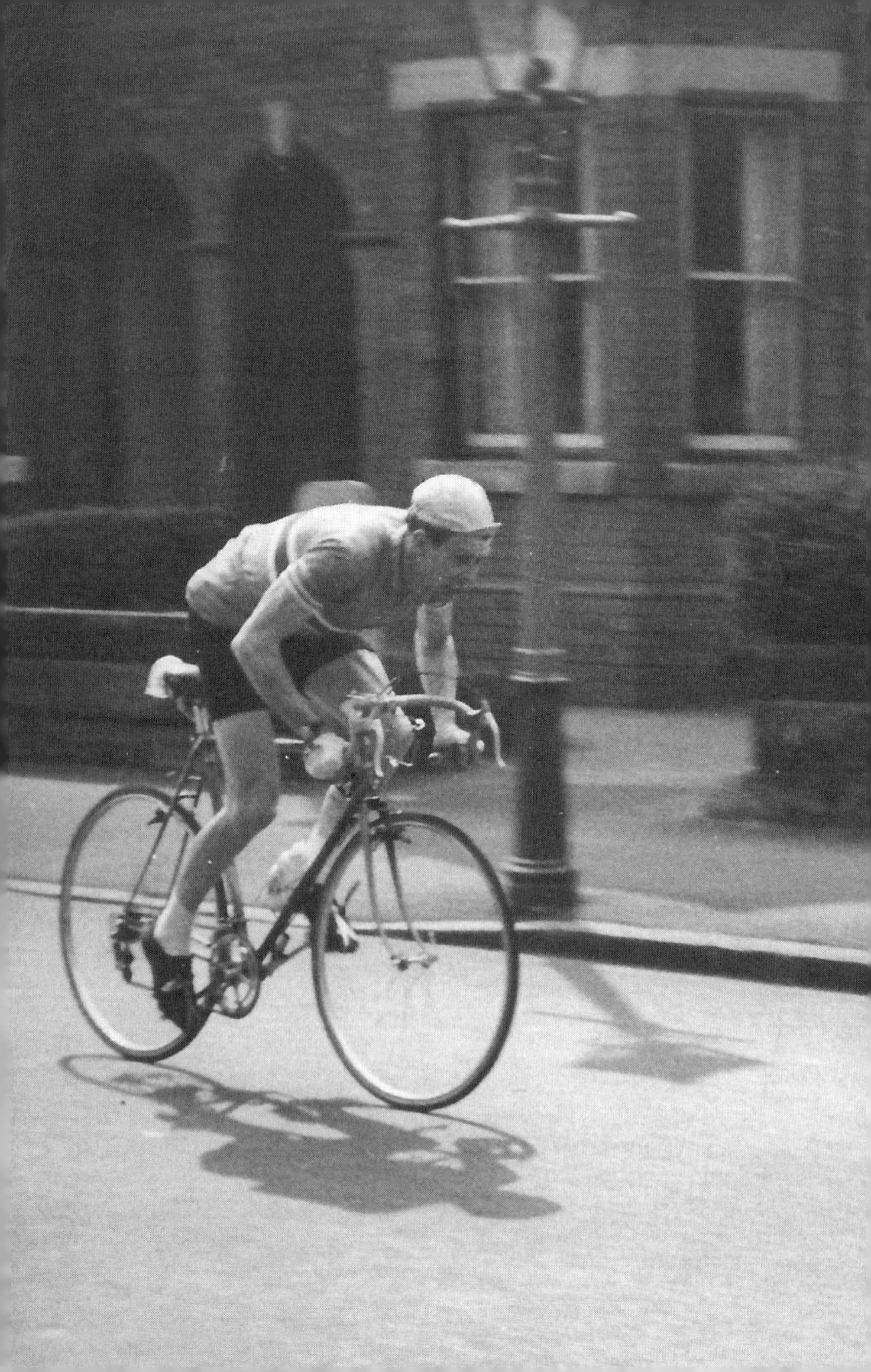

CHAPTER 9

TACTICS

I have mentioned road racing and brains, earlier in the book, and you may say that what I have told you up to now comes with experience and common sense. I will reply by saying that if riders did all I have mentioned previously, there would be a fantastic improvement in racing. I have seen some top riders who did not know how to change or work efficiently. Some of this chapter is very difficult to explain and is rarely seen in action, except in the broadest sense, in this country.

I am often asked, 'Why do you work with rival teams?' I also hear people shouting 'Number 24 is winning', because he is in front as he passes by with twenty miles to go. When I won a stage in an important race after being in a breakaway for over sixty miles, a chap came up to us in the hotel afterwards and said, 'I suppose you are all pals together and just sprint at the finish to please the crowd'. These remarks show how uneducated the general public is when it comes to our sport.

Of course, it would be ideal if you could breakaway with just your own team, but I have never seen this happen. The reason is obvious, forty hostile rivals in the bunch are not going to sit back and watch four members of the same team ride away. Four against forty are big odds. But when eight riders from six different teams pull away, then sixteen riders are left defending them in the bunch, and the odds are far better.

When people try to eliminate tactics from road racing, I get really annoyed. Some do it thinking it will make races faster, by stopping lazy riders sitting idle in the bunch with the excuse that they have a team mate away in the breakaway. This is wrong; to defend a team mate properly is really an exhausting task. A lazy rider does not need an excuse and will shirk with or without a team.

If a person does not like tactics then time-trials are more in his line. The Australian handicap road races, are the type to encourage juniors and third category riders to ride flat out.

A lowly placed rider can get a great deal of satisfaction and hard work defending and helping a leading team mate, or trying for a team win.

Nearly all tactics in cycle racing are formed round wind resistance, acceleration and climbing ability. Here are some figures to illustrate the drastic effect of wind resistance in still air, showing the vital importance of a streamlined position.

DRAG

Medium size man, height 5 feet 10 inches, weight 150 lbs.

Drag Area in:

Speed Approx.	Racing Posn.	Touring Posn.	Track Posn.
45 ft./Sec.	3.3 sq. ft.	3.9 sq. ft.	3.12 sq. ft.

Drag area of cycle alone — 1 sq. ft. (very high)
Jacket and flannels increased his drag area by 30%

Distance Miles	Time			Mean Speed m.p.h.	Average Power needed to overcome		
	hrs.	mins.	sec.		Friction	Air Drag	Total Resis.
10		23	17	25.72	0.062	0.389	0.451
25		59	52	25.05	0.060	0.351	0.411
30	1	14	15	24.24	0.058	0.318	0.376
50	2	7	12	23.43	0.056	0.294	0.350
100	4	30	52	22.15	0.053	0.248	0.301

TACTICS

RIDING IN ECHELON

Small group, echelon formation –
direction of change, wind from right.

A

B

C

D

Small group, echelon formation –
direction of change, wind from extreme right.

A

B

C

D

KING OF SPORTS

Small group, echelon formation –
direction of change, wind from left.

A

B

C

D

Small group, echelon formation –
direction of change, wind from front or no wind.

A

B

C

D

TACTICS

Taking a right hand bend when all is clear behind

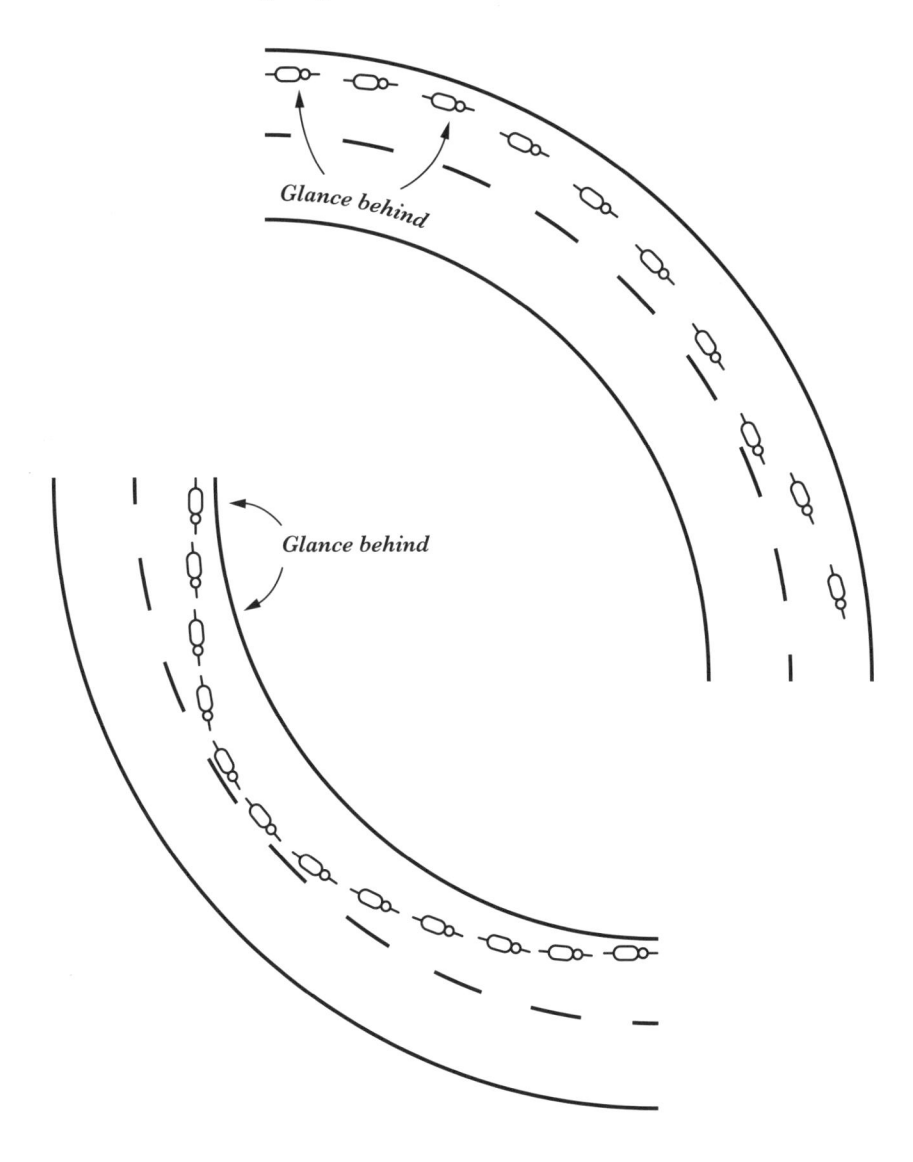

Glance behind

Glance behind

Taking a left hand bend when all is clear behind

KING OF SPORTS

The bunch correctly echeloned. Wind blowing from the right.
Only riders in black unprotected.

WIND

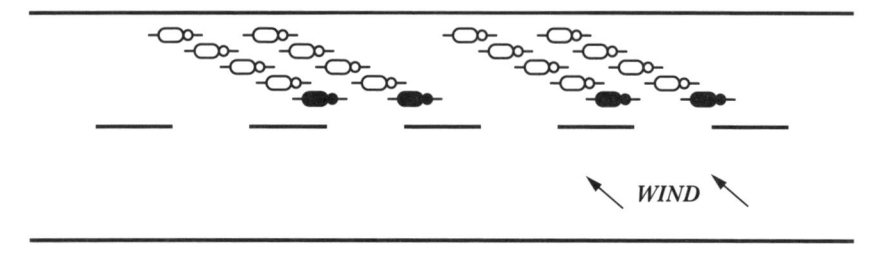

Large breakaway correctly echeloned.
Only riders in black unprotected.

WIND

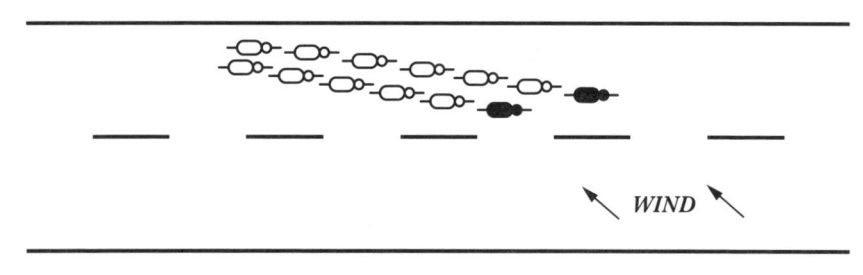

Bunch incorrectly echeloned. All riders in black unprotected.

WIND

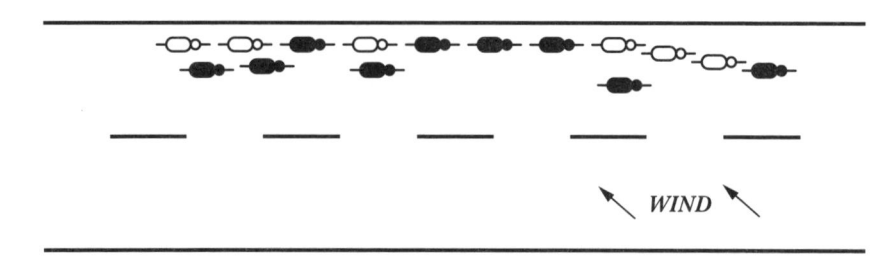

TACTICS

Large breakaway incorrectly echeloned.
All riders in black unprotected.

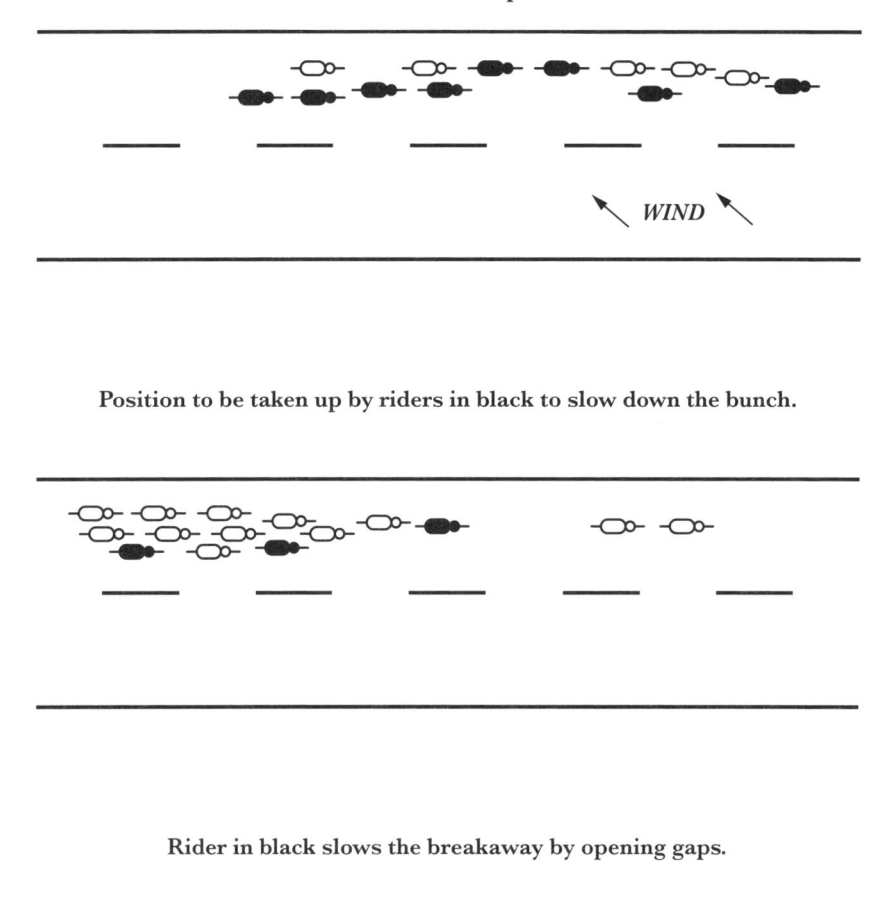

WIND

Position to be taken up by riders in black to slow down the bunch.

Rider in black slows the breakaway by opening gaps.

When you note how a cyclist can do 40 m.p.h. behind the slim shelter of a motorcycle for quite long periods, you realise what a difference a windbreak makes. Wind resistance is a great deal more than all the functional resistances of your bike put together.

Acceleration takes a great deal more effort than maintaining a steady pace; the further the race has gone on, the harder it becomes.

Climbing is usually a natural phenomenon. Some people can improve with training whilst other riders who are good in other parts of the course learn to hang on during the climbs. Usually, the hill climber lacks something in other parts of his cycling make-up, and doesn't often win many races.

HOW TO SLOW DOWN THE BUNCH

Before you and your team try this, make sure the end justifies the means and you are not wasting energy for nothing. When you see your efforts are not having any effect after a hard try, then pack it in and save your energy.

When do the bunch need slowing down? If your best man or men are in a breakaway and they stand a good chance; if your best man is off the back in a stage race or, in a long single stage event, has a puncture.

When you have three men in the bunch, then two should move up nearly to the front and the third man should move about halfway along the bunch on the outside. FIG. 22. The front two should position themselves alternately behind the leading bunch riders. Every time the front rider moves for someone to come through, one of your riders should overtake slowly (not too slowly so as to make it obvious, but slowly enough to cut down the rhythm and pace of the bunch). Every other time there is a change at the front one of the team should be there to keep the pace down. The third rider should be watching and joining anyone trying to escape from the bunch by accelerating down the side of the bunch and coming past the front riders too fast for them to catch him. Then he should slow them down as I shall describe in 'slowing the breakaway'.

It may seem that such action could not slow down a bunch enough, but when you remember how smoothly the breakaway must work in order to gain seconds, you realise a bunch needs equally the same smooth action to bring it back. If gaps keep opening and the pace keeps slowing in the bunch, the break will soon be uncatchable. Do not defend energetically a rider who is obviously not strong

TACTICS

enough to win, or a silly but strong teammate who is battling a head wind on his own with a long way to the finish.

In the last stage of a 5-day race one of our teammates was lying in about 6th place on general classification and about 4 minutes down from the race leader, National Road Race Champion, Derek Evans. The position seemed impossible but we decided we would give our rider the best chance we could.

After 20 miles, a break group with nobody of importance went away and my teammate moved up to join it. Three of us slowed down the bunch as I have described previously. However, due to frequent attacks of the worried race leaders, the group gained little ground. Our next move was to let through one by one, as if by accident, some of the good riders who were behind our leading teammate on general classification. Soon the reinforced break gained ground and disappeared. Our effort still continued in the bunch and we finished an incredible 10 minutes behind. Our rider, unfortunately, did not win having been dropped by the break with 12 miles to go, but we had given him every chance. Sometimes you may be helped by another team who also have a good teammate away.

An incident which occurred in a single stage race; two powerful teams, to one of which I belonged, dominated the event. After 40 miles and with 40 to go, following much attacking by both teams, one rider from each team pulled away from the bunch in a break of four. Both major teams defended and soon the bunch was under their control and in ten miles the lead jumped to four minutes.

Our man in the break was a good rider but previous events had shown that he tended to fade with ten miles to go. With this in mind, I decided to close the gap to a smaller margin so that I could be in a better position. When I started whipping up the pace, riders looked amazed at me trying to catch my own teammate. Once I had cut the lead down to two minutes, I kept this constant. Then, with fifteen miles to go, we caught my exhausted teammate who had been left by our rivals in the breakaway. After a hard chase, we caught the leaders with four miles to go, proving that you should know your team and ride your race accordingly.

HOW TO SLOW THE BREAKAWAY

Again, be sure your reasons are good and that you are not making a nuisance of yourself. Good reasons are:

(i) You know you are not good enough to beat the riders in the break but your teammate, who is in the bunch, is.

(ii) Your team have a good chance of a team-win but your most dangerous rivals have more men in the break than you and are capable of staying with it.

(iii) Your best teammate is out in front on his own or with a small group and it is not far to the finish.

It is more difficult to slow a break because your intentions are more obvious when you are in a small group, so don't bother trying to disguise them.

Try and get in front of the weakest rider who will find it difficu to close the gaps you keep letting open at every opportunity. Ease up slowly in the middle of the group, slow the riders behind and let one or two riders in front go. This will cause the rider behind you to pull out and close the gap you have left. If the wind is blowing, keep swinging the group when you are at the front in the wrong direction for their protection but remember, and this is important, never dangerously obstruct a rider. You must rely on spoiling the rhythm regularly until you disrupt and demoralise the opposition. Fig. 23 shows.

COUNTER TACTICS

Of course, for every attack there is a defence, and the problem is organising it. You must be ever watchful of someone trying the previous tactics on you or your team. The best method, if your breakaway is being slowed by a defensive rider, is for each rider to cut in front of the offender and keep him at the back. If he will not budge then, either try to place yourself behind the defending rider so that when he slows you go straight past and nullify any slowing effect. Warn other riders and tell them to go through if they slow behind the culprit. If you are in the break and the defending is too effective and the other riders will not co-operate in overcoming it, do not work yourself to death, but wait for the bunch and try again later. Do not try to take the defensive riders next time. Should a lazy or defensive rider just sit at the back of the group, waiting to flash past at the finish, you must combine against him.

I have often noticed riders (particularly Continental riders) getting away with lazy riding in a breakaway either by staying at the back or doing their bit at the front slower and shorter than the other riders who are fighting to establish a lead. Baldini in the I.O.M. and Uriona in the Tour of Britain did this for no apparently honourable reason and won. If you are in a break in which riders are refusing to work and you cannot bully them into action then you must get rid of them. This is done by every rider in the group taking turns at letting the breakaway go while he slows down the offender only behind him. To stay in the group the lazy rider will have to keep closing the gap time after time. Soon he will either tire and drop out or decide it is easier to work with the rest. It is silly to work hard with the knowledge that someone who has had an easy ride will beat you at the finish.

When defensive riders are causing havoc with the speed of the bunch, and the break you wish to catch is gaining fast, try and organise a group to nullify the effect as above. Should this fail, the only thing to do is to get a few of the remaining good riders to join you in a vicious, fast attack down the outside of the bunch. You must hope speed will keep the defenders off your tail.

When the bunch is working reasonably well and making some impression on the breakaway, don't be stupid and take a flyer to bridge the gap on your own; instead use your energy sensibly by working with the bunch in a chasing group. Riders selfishly using this technique, often fail to bridge the gap alone and disrupt the smooth working of the riders in the chasing group.

When your efforts fail don't just give up, try and think of a different method. Stablinski won the French championships by attacking on the last rise before the finish, when his rival changed gear and was off guard.

I caused a breakaway to lose ground when all else had failed, by waiting until ten miles to the finish and then attacking in short bursts. The other riders – frightened that I might win, after having an easy ride defending my yellow-jersied teammate behind – began to chase me. When I was caught, I eased. When the group re-organised, I jumped again – and so on. These tactics lost the breakaway two minutes in those few final miles.

Although I have only seen a few cases, the bad practice of jersey-pulling in tight sprints, should be severely punished. It is certainly not good tactics, it is dangerous and can be used to give a lever in a sprint – very unfair.

HOW TO APPLY TACTICS

Let's assume that you have one man in your team capable of winning and that the rest of your team are reasonably fit. Your leading rider has already told the rest of the team the names of the four of five men he fears most. Also, at what distance and where he thinks it would benefit him to break away. If he is a 'stamina' man it will be early on, but not until after 20 miles, unless two or more top riders attack and make it impossible for him to stay behind. The reason he should not attack early, as a rule, is because every rider in the field fit or unfit, is raring to go in the first ten to fifteen miles. Should only one of the top riders go, one of your teammates should join the group as quickly as possible and slow it down.

If your man has to start an attack on his own, as we have already said, he stands a chance of winning, it is not likely that the other top riders will let him go on his own. Unless there is some defensive work going on he should join with his best teammate and move to the outside near the back of the bunch without trying to conceal it too much. Continue slowly down the outside until, glancing behind, he sees three riders or so are on his wheel. Then, in a gear slightly higher than normal, he should accelerate down the bunch and flat out fly past the front riders. For 200 yards he should keep going and then move across into the wind and let his teammate or the next man come through. A quick glance behind should inform him of the situation. If the bunch is right behind, give up, but if they are stretched in a long line, keep going even faster for a while and see if the line will snap.

Should the bunch stay intact not bothering to chase, keep going fast, changing quickly until out of sight.

This is what he should be thinking about besides keeping the break moving. There is a long way to go; so the break must consist of either seven or more riders of reasonable class, or over four of very good class. If the break does not match up to the qualities above, then there are two alternatives, one being to drop back to the bunch before wasting more energy, and the other being to ride steadily in the break not using any undue effort and using it as a stepping-stone

TACTICS

to the next break that comes along. It is useless for him to charge along in a hopeless break and after a while to find that he is out on his own, shattered, with a bunch on his heels.

When the best team rider is a climber, he will of course initiate attacks on the climbs. Firstly, a teammate, if available, will make the pace fast at the front of the bunch for the first half of the climb. Then the No. 1 man will attack – not so fast that he goes away on his own, but fast enough to enable only a compact group go with him. It is silly for a climber to cross the summit alone, without help and still 40 miles to go. If your climber lacks stamina, he should only attack on the climbs near the end of the race.

The rider who likes to go later in the race (often the sprinter-type) has a great deal to watch and should have a great deal of confidence in his judgment. He must watch every break that goes and note its riders. If any of the top men he has noted go with a breakaway, he must, if possible, send a teammate to break it up. When he has no teammates, he must let it go. Only when two or more of his feared rivals go together later in the race must he join them. His teammate, if he has any should lead him out from the bunch with all the speed he has to as near the break as possible, if it is already away. But remember, the decision to chase must be instantaneous or not at all, every second wasted, deciding whether or not to chase, means extra hard work to catch up.

No matter how good you are, to try and go with every break is silly and probably when the right one comes along you will be so tired after working with the failures, you will either not have the speed to join it, or the energy to stay with it. It is the top riders who make the running in 90% of the cases. If the race has one outstanding rider then try to breakaway with a group of good riders. Then the top man's chase to catch you may make him easier to handle.

Team victory is something similar. You must watch only the riders whom you consider are dangerous to your team and those who are likely to win the race. If your opposition send two men away in a break which has no outstanding men in it and which you don't think has much chance, let them go and wear themselves out. Try and get two of your riders in any group which has the top riders in it because, even should they get dropped near the finish, they will probably beat the bunch in and give you a valuable lead.

Always enquire which method the organisers are using to select the team winners, e.g. last man home, average time, etc., so that you know what to aim for.

When you are in a breakaway, try and keep the group together until you are well clear and only have about ten miles to go. The more riders in a break the more the work is spread out. Of course, if the bunch are breathing down your necks stay together, if possible, to the finish. It is better to finish 5th in the break than 20th in the bunch.

If you are in a large group, whittle it down by a few sharp increases in pace or a bit of fast climbing on any good gradients on the course. When it is reduced to five or six riders who are perhaps nearly as good as yourself and with only five miles to go, start breaking up the remainder by team tactics.

One of you should attack suddenly from the back of the group, choosing a good place, e.g. the bottom of a small descent and start of a small incline, when those in front are changing gear and are unsuspecting. Your teammate must know what you are going to do so that he is ready and can catch the wheel or shelter of the first man to give chase. When this man swings out, your team should ease and come through slowly, using the tactics I have described earlier.

If the chasing men catch you, your teammate should attack as soon as you are getting shelter. This should continue only if you see that what is left of the break is thinning out and getting slower at pulling you back, until finally one of you pulls away.

Note that whilst you are defending, you can cause havoc to the group by passive riding so that when it is your turn to attack you are ready.

When you are the only representative of your team in a breakaway group getting the above treatment from another team your answer lies in riding with the other individuals in your group as a team, each man marking the wheel of one of the attacking team. If your man breaks clear, taking you with him, you must keep your trust and not work with him, otherwise, if you are caught, none of the lone riders in the group will trust you and you will be back where you started – rivals working against team effort.

Should you be on your own, or have poor team support, and the breakaway group you are in is approaching the later parts of the race, you should have the opposition weighed up. If you are a climber, and have not a finishing burst, and in the group is a sprinter, it is no good praying that he will puncture. You must get rid of him before the finishing straight. Do not let your mind convince you, 'Well, he might tire or puncture before the finish; I'll wait and see'. Make the pace fast and when the last hill or terrain you consider to be your favourite arrives, you must attack with everything you've got and attack again and again until you drop him.

TACTICS

If this does not succeed, then about a half mile from the finish you must put every last ounce into a long sprint. Should he get your wheel, ease immediately; it's useless, unless the rider is tiring and you are climbing, to try to drop anyone off your wheel – try again later. Should he win after all this, take your hat off to a better man, but at least you tried harder than you would by sitting in all the way and waiting for him to sweep past you at the finish.

When you know there is only a quarter of a mile to go and it is a sprint finish, remember how you sprint best in your training and carry it out here. Try and have a look at the finish before the race starts, or find out about it from the organiser. Ask especially about its gradient, whether up or down if it is narrow or wide and if there are any sharp corners in the last 400 yards.

Use a higher gear than normal, but do not overgear; your training sprints should be your guide. Note which way the wind (if at all strong) is blowing and try to sprint down the sheltered side of the group. If you have a teammate in the group, the poorer sprinter should lead out. When you prefer a long sprint go at the point you found was best in training, trying perhaps to use a slow patch when the other riders are jostling for position.

Should you enjoy a short sprint, make sure you are near the front of the group and stay there. Never take the lead but try to get right behind a strong sprinter, or your teammate if he is strong enough. Suddenly – usually at about 300 yards to go, after a few false alarms – the group will surge forward faster and faster, so hold your man close as he accelerates. Let him break the wind and pull you through past the other riders. Then, with not less than 100 yards to go, you must move out and pass him if you are to win.

Tommy Simpson becomes World Champion, 1965.

CHAPTER 10
STAGE EVENTS

I have heard riders, after Tours of Britain, complain about three main things: the length of the stages, the inclusion of poor roads and the long hard climbs. The latter two I dismiss because, on the Continent, the roads are worse and the climbs far longer. The former, I believe, should be attended to quickly. The Warsaw—Berlin—Prague top amateur stage race rarely has stages over 100 miles. Our stages should average 80 miles.

One of the most exciting and fastest stages I have ever ridden was the one from Edinburgh to Glasgow – won by Des. Robinson (Brian Robinson's brother). The stage was only 70 miles, and I don't remember changing below 96in. gear from start to finish.

If the Continental amateurs, with all their time to train, average small distances in stage races, it is common sense that our full-time, working amateurs must have the stage distance cut.

Shorter, faster stages would, I believe, build up our riders during races like the Tour of Britain instead of breaking down promising riders.

In well sponsored events the prizes should be spread out more than they are at present.

Hotels are one of the biggest causes of trouble in a stage race. Many boarding houses tend to cash in on a tour. I have seen six riders crammed into a double room and each given a boiled egg for breakfast. Two-star hotels often charge riders extra, but treat them as second class guests with third class appetites. Four star hotels who are used to handling even eccentric people with courtesy, charge no extra and generally treat cyclists in a first class manner.

Every effort should be made to enable the stages to be finished with a few laps of a small circuit. This would enable the crowds to see something of the race.

Guest celebrities, programme lotteries and photographic prizes stimulate public interest.

TEAM MANAGER

In stage races the team manager and mechanic play a vital role. The manager should discuss the race with all the riders in his team before the first stage and every evening after that.

Well before the race starts he should check what his assistants are like and inform them how the work will be split between them. Then if one of them will not co-operate he will have time to find a replacement.

Sometimes a temperamental masseur wants to give the riders a quick rub down and finish early. Once a lazy mechanic went to the pictures in the evening, overslept and left the race leader to start on a buckled wheel.

The manager must discuss how the teams' winnings are to be split, including between himself and his helpers. He should try to keep the team pulling as one. Unless he is an ace manager, he should not try to direct policy, but rather listen to the riders' ideas and sort out the best ones.

He must be able to boost the riders' morale and ensure no riders are allowed to feel left out and neglected.

A team captain should be chosen to direct riding during the race. This does not need to be the leading rider of the team, but the most intelligent and experienced rider.

A good authoritative team captain is a major asset to any team. Riders are naturally reluctant to stop when a team is delayed with trouble, or to slow down the bunch when a teammate is in a good breakaway (one they wish they were in themselves). Your team captain is the man-on-the-spot, who can organise the team to deal with situations as they arise.

The manager should ensure that everything is looked after: all his riders are ready to move off three quarters of an hour before the start; they have all their special food and drinks with them; their main baggage is ready for dispatch (or he has it himself); he has all spare bottles and mussettes labelled and packed with what each rider wants at the feeding station; the team car or van is tidy with everything in its place, with wheels and tools easily accessible and spare bikes are secure, but can be quickly removed. Tyres on all spare bikes and wheels should be stuck on, pumped up and not chaffing. He should note the weather forecast and tell the riders what conditions are likely and which way the wind is blowing.

At the start he should collect all the tracksuits and put one in each rider's individual bag. He should tell the boys which side of the road he will be feeding

STAGE EVENTS

on and what he will be wearing. He ought to wear a big red hat or yellow jacket so that his riders will easily pick him out at the feeding station. He must feed each rider; so should warn his team to spread out so he has time to get to each one if there is a bunch of riders. He should leave his mechanic or assistant at the end of his station with a couple of mussettes in case any rider misses him.

While the race is in progress he should plan and decide how he will deal with every situation, from crashes to punctures; above all he should always stay calm.

I have seen Stan Britain puncture twice in one stage and change bikes four times, yet it was sorted out so quickly by his team manager, Eddie Soens, that he never went off the back of the bunch. When he punctured, up went his hand, his team car rushed 300 yards in front of the bunch, the mechanic jumped out with a spare machine, Stan changed bikes and was off again before the last man in the bunch passed him.

Of course, the team manager's main interest must be his highly placed riders, but he should always try and help the others quickly if they are in trouble. If he gets to the finish before the riders, he should find out where the washrooms or their hotels are, so that as soon as they finish, he can hand them their bags, direct them, and off they can go.

Some tepal or grease remover is ideal to clean the black and greasy baths riders leave. I often think this must put more hotels 'off' riders than anything else.

At their hotel he should tell them what time dinner is and find out a good place for them to get a good meal later.

Riders need two evening meals on a stage race. Looking for a cafe for a decent late meal wastes valuable time. Approach the manager of the hotel as soon as you book in, to see if he can provide you with the late, extra meal.

Check with the hotel chef and make the best of the meals he has available. See if he can arrange a none-fried breakfast. Should the following day be hard, the team manager should visit the butcher and supply his own steaks to the chef as an extra for his team's breakfast. Either he, the mechanic or the masseur should do any special shopping, i.e. special food, embrocation, equipment etc. He should collect the riders' laundry, if required and tell them the time of the team meeting. Afterwards if he has time he should see if he can help the mechanic.

His job is a hard one and it covers the range from diplomacy to mother love. Once the riders have raced and are tired and edgy it is his job to calm and look after them, to ensure that they get as much rest as possible.

Many managers go on stage races with the idea of the cigar smoking continental director sportif fixed in their minds. They forget that this man is usually a director and has two or three mechanics, a couple of masseurs and one or two errand boys on his pay roll. Our managers will be lucky to have one mechanic and one masseur to look after five or seven riders. He must be prepared to roll up his sleeves and give a helping hand. I have been annoyed, on several Tours on seeing a few managers going 'out on the town', leaving the mechanic bogged down with work and the riders without transport to get them to the late evening meal.

STAGE EVENTS
MECHANICS' CHECKLIST

Make of cycle ....

Name ....

Any special faults to be checked ....

Any gear ratio changes ....

Front Wheel
Rim true & no spokes broken ☐
Free running, no excessive play ☐
Tyre, no flints & good tread ☐
Tyre secure ☐
Tyre saver O.K. ☐

Rear Wheel
Rim true & no spokes broken ☐
Free running, no excessive play ☐
Tyre, no flints and good tread ☐
Tyre secure ☐
Tyre saver O.K. ☐

Brakes
Free operation ☐
Blocks fitting true on rims ☐
Blocks good ☐
Adjustment O.K. ☐
All nuts tight, lever secure. ☐

Gears
Operating over full range ☐
Cables not frayed ☐
Jockey wheels free ☐

KING OF SPORTS

Levers reasonably frictioned ☐
All nuts tight ☐
Chain no stiff links ☐

Bottom Bracket
Cotters or cotterless tight ☐
All nuts on chain wheel tight ☐
Bracket locking ring tight ☐
Chain wheel side B.B. cup tight ☐
Free yet no excessive play on spindle ☐

Head Set
Locknuts tight ☐
Free but no excessive play ☐
Extension bolt tight ☐
Handlebar secure ☐

Seat
Pillar bolt tight ☐
Saddle tight ☐

Pedals
Secure to cranks ☐
Locknut tight ☐
Free but no excessive play ☐
Clips secure ☐
Straps unchafed ☐

Accessories
Pump ☐
Spare tyre secure ☐
Pressure pump secure ☐
Bottle cage secure ☐
Cycle clean ☐
All parts oiled ☐

STAGE EVENTS
THE MECHANIC

The mechanic's job is also hard. Not only must he be alert throughout the race, at the end of the race his job really starts.

He should write to riders before the race starts and say what he expects of them. Machines should be clean and in perfect condition at the start. Any damaged or faulty item on their cycles should be ready to be changed without having to chase around to ask permission. Payment should be made as soon as possible for these items. Mountain ratio gears should be on the spare wheel. No late requested changes should be carried out after six o'clock. The tallest and smallest riders should bring spare machines. Each rider should provide a complete list of their equipment and take at least one spare of each item liable to damage. The mechanic should ensure he gets to know the workings of any unfamiliar piece of equipment and make sure he has all the various shaped tools for cotterless cranks, etc. He should bring a stand to hang the cycles on while they are cleaned and the gear functioning is checked. A vice fastened on a long piece of wood or metal is also a must.

If he can get hold of all the machines a couple of days before the race he should try and make them so that any wheel can be interchanged and will fit easily, with all gears working, from frame to frame.

As soon as the riders have changed after the stage, he should find out from each rider if anything on his machine has been giving trouble, any changes of gearing etc. and note them down. A sheet as set out on previous pages, filled in by each rider saves anything being forgotten. He must never go to bed leaving something for the morning, no matter how small it may seem.

The mechanic should start off by cleaning every bike, taking plenty of rags and some good hand cleaner for afterwards. This not only keeps the job cleaner, but nothing is worse, psychologically, for a rider than to start off on a dirty machine. Then he must check the tubular tyres, change any that are worn or badly cut, remove all flints, etc. from the tread and check that they are still stuck on securely, especially after rain. Then he must go through the list of snags or changes requested by the riders. When these are cured he should carefully check each machine.

Finally, he must ride round on any machine on which he has carried out any alterations on. Then he can go to bed with the grand feeling that everything is ready. If he is lucky and finishes early or has nothing to do at any time he should see if he can give the manager a hand.

THE MASSEUR

The good masseur's job is a hard one, but only for two periods each day. Therefore he must be prepared to give a hand with the more menial tasks with a good heart when the team officials number only three.

We once had a Swedish masseur who helped to carry the riders' luggage; cleaned the riders' shoes, bottles, caps and socks; trimmed the riders' nails and gave them eye baths. In doing these tasks he did not neglect his main job and each rider was given a thorough massage from finger-tips to toes.

Sooner than take a non-co-operative mediocre masseur with me, if I was a manager, I would learn how to apply massage myself, and take along a willing odd job man to give a hand.

The masseur should take with him a medical kit, rather more comprehensive than that I list for the riders.

I have seen a good masseur give a down and out rider such a psychological build up that he has won the next stage of a big race.

A good co-operative masseur is worth his weight in gold, an idle one causes so much friction he is not worth taking (when he is one of a few officials on a stage race).

CHAPTER 11

PREPARING TO RIDE IN A STAGE RACE

PREPARATION OF YOURSELF

Never accept an invitation for a stage race unless you are really fit or have time to get fit. If you ride out of condition, not only will you have a grueling and miserable ride yourself but, should one of your teammates either become race leader or get into a position to attack him, you will not be in a fit state to give your colleague your much-needed assistance. Ensure you have had an anti-tetanus injection. Your early season stamina miles should be your main back up. Build up your form as the season progresses. Early season race winners rarely last.

About two months before the race, build up your stamina by increasing slightly the length of your training runs on two nights per week and increase your sleep on the corresponding night. On one other evening do twenty or so miles fast to prevent your stamina-building runs from taking the edge off your speed. Be careful you do not get over-enthusiastic and do too much. Use your weekend races as a guide to your form. Eat more protein foods and vitamin pills. Harden your backside and feet night and morning with surgical spirit. Have a medical and dental check-up a month before the race. Teeth suffer through eating lots of sweet food during the race, and there is enough suffering without toothache.

PREPARATION OF YOUR MACHINE

Start at least three weeks before the event. Check cones, spindles and bearings for wear. Re-grease all bearing surfaces. Before a long or important stage renew chain, sprockets, gear cables and brake blocks. If all the team ride newish but well run-in chains and sprockets it will prevent chains slipping if wheels are inter-changed from one machine to another. Ensure that when your spare wheel is fitted your gear does not need readjusting. This can be done either by packing washers behind the block or by spacing washers on the block side of the spindle if the blocks do not line up exactly. If the race has any hilly stages, fit a wide ratio block to your spare wheel. This will save your hard-worked mechanic from messing about changing rings and sprockets during the race. All he will do is change your rear wheel.

Check if your cycling shoes need repairing. If they do, get it done as soon as possible. Walk round in them during the evenings to wear them in. Change the laces. Check your shoe plates for wear and ensure they are firmly fixed to the shoes.

Slacken off your saddle slightly to make it softer. I personally find it more comfortable if the stem is raised a quarter of an inch and the saddle pillar lowered one eighth of an inch.

WHAT TO TAKE ON A RACE LASTING OVER SIX DAYS

MEDICAL
Embrocation
Wintergreen
Petroleum Jelly
Surgical spirit
Eye wash (mainly when abroad)
Elastoplast quarter inch roll
Tin of Elastoplast
Back Plasters
Sun Cream
Olive Oil
Vitamin Pills
Protein Supplement
Honey
Aspirins
Digestive tablets
Mild sleeping pills
Foot ointment or Paraffin Wax
Tube of Setavlex (for saddle boils)

CLOTHING
2 pairs of cycling shoes
4/8 pairs white ankle socks
3 pairs racing shorts
2 long sleeved pullovers
Track suit & mitts
2 spare racing vests & 3 team racing vests
Waterproofs (racing)
3 racing caps
Crash Helmet (a must in many countries)
Braces
Ordinary gloves
Shoes and slippers
2 pairs 'U' pants
4 vests
2 pairs ordinary socks
3 shirts and a tie
Trousers
Sports Jacket & a Plastic Raincoat
4 handkerchiefs

EXTRAS

Razor, toothbrush and paste, shoe polish and brush, soap and three towels, large sponge and sponge bag, bath salts, sunglasses and goggles, comb and hair cream, needle and cotton, racing license, small bag for track suit etc., 4 spare tubulars (as new), any special tools for cotterless cranks etc., spare feeding bottles.

DURING STAGE RACE, AT LEISURE

Do not pick out any one of your team to be your main hope as it is surprising how some people below form at the beginning of a stage race can ride themselves in.

Agree before the race starts, to split your winnings, if any, on a percentage basis. The rider who wins the most and the one who helped the most should receive the biggest shares. It is unfair that the man who rode himself into the ground for a high placed teammate, should be rewarded the same as a shirker who kept out of the way when required and only worked when told, or to gain an advantage for himself.

Plan your evenings and mornings carefully and try to follow a strict and time saving routine. Note down the names and addresses of all your hotels on a label and tie it to the kit bag carrying your track suit.

Immediately after finishing the stage, pick up your bag from the team car and without hanging about go to your hotel. Have a bath (before the other riders get in) and then go to bed for at least an hour before dinner.

After dinner sort out your kit for morning, clothing, food, and bottles. Wash any items such as socks and feeding bottles and clean your shoes. The masseur often does this job in the continent, and also carries the riders' heavy bags to and from their rooms. Rest again and then with the team manager and your teammates discuss the tactics for the following stage, and the chances of the team and of your better placed riders.

Should any riders in your team have employed any bad tactics or avoided helping, point out to him what you think should have been done. Do not wait until these mistakes build up into a major team crisis – discuss each problem as it arises.

Take special care not to form any cliques which could make riders feel left out; especially riders who are not riding well.

Afterwards go for your second evening meal; do not sit around too long talking after the meal; get back to your hotel instead and do some deep breathing exercises, one or two yoga relaxing exercises, then have a massage and go to bed as early as possible. A pillow under the knees often helps to relax tired legs.

In the morning allow yourself ample time. Put your racing clothing on under your tracksuit. Your cycling shoes should be put on just before proceeding to the start. Pack your main suitcase and kit bag before breakfast. In your kit bag put socks, vest, shirt, waterproof, food, embrocation wintergreen, sunglasses or goggles, track mitts, cap, cycling shoes, towel, soap and spare sweater. Give yourself time to eat a leisurely and hearty breakfast. Rest again for at least half an hour, have a massage. Then with three quarters of an hour to the 'off' pick up your kit bag and make your way to the start, checking your machine as you go.

I suffer badly from aching and burning feet in long races. I have tried all sorts of remedies but I find the best is to thickly coat the balls of the feet and under the toes with paraffin wax or Vaseline.

DURING THE RACE, AT WORK

Always try to keep near the front half of the bunch so you can keep an eye on what is going on. On windy days always fight to get in the front echelon or form a second one. At all costs keep out of the gutter line of riders for nothing is more fatiguing and soul destroying in stage racing. On the Continent several echelons are formed, but in England riders are generally so thoughtless that they either want to be in the front echelon or not in one at all.

Be especially careful about the breaks you go with. It is no use pulling away, early on a long stage, with seven riders or less, or working too hard, because even if you manage to keep away until the finish you will have taken so much out of yourself that you may not last through the other stages.

Constantly be on the alert and conserve your energy as much as possible by keeping towards the front of the bunch, closing gaps as quickly as possible, sheltering close to and on the correct side of the rider in front.

Watch out near the end of a stage for riders 'creeping away' to gain some time and join them if possible. Sometimes these late breakaways over the last few miles gain as much time as others which have been away nearly all the stage and exerting far more energy.

PREPARING TO RIDE IN A STAGE RACE

Do not carry shirking riders on the back of your breakaway; shake them off. Even if the shirker does not win today, he will be rested enough to attack you tomorrow.

Try and vary your racing diet slightly each day. I often take a chicken leg, or something tasty like a peach, or bar of turkish delight (a delightful change from what can become a dreary racing diet, after about four days). Eat well during the long stages and spread your drinking to last out the stage comfortably. Never rely too much on a bottle or food at a feeding station because in the general confusion you might miss it. It is always advisable to carry extra, just in case.

When riders lose over 15 minutes on the race leader, they must be prepared to sacrifice themselves for the rest of the team. They should give their bike or wheels in case of mechanical trouble, slow down breakaways their leading teammates are not in, help their leading teammates bridge the gap to a dangerous-looking break and slow the bunch down when their teammates are away.

When you lose time and become a domestic do not despair and think that the race is over for you. It is not. You can really start to enjoy the race, without any of the worries or cares of the leading riders. When your team is in trouble, you can pitch into the battle with everything you've got. You need not worry unduly about the problems facing the highly placed riders (e.g. am I using too much energy? Will I blow up? Will we catch the breakaway?) Even so, you can still pick up many prime and stage prizes because a lowly placed rider does not warrant the constant vigilance of the top riders.

I have gained more satisfaction and enjoyment in helping a team mate to win the Tour of Britain than in finishing in sixth place myself.

Half-way through a 'Tour of Britain' I have witnessed, two either selfish or dim riders working with a strong breakaway group when their yellow jerseyed teammate was back in the bunch. This was not their only blunder because our team had four riders in the break, and at the end of the stage we had the race leader and were the leading team.

If you gain race leadership in the first quarter of the race, do not fight to keep it unless you are either superior to the other competitors or you are a climber and the following stages are hilly. The reason for this is that usually, early in the race too many riders are within striking distance, and to attack or watch them all would take too much out of you and your team. Once the bunch sees that you are defending your leader's jersey they will 'sit on the wheels' of you or your mates whenever a breakaway goes or a gap opens, knowing that you will close it to keep your position. This is an exasperating and exhausting situation.

I recall in one of the 'Circuits of Britain' when I started a third stage with over seven minutes lead on my nearest rivals. I had a weak team and I could not match every move. At first, I tried attacking but the stage was flat and no one would work with the race leader. Once I was away with a group of riders who were lying second in the team placing but with no one highly placed individually. They stupidly also had yellow jersey blues and would not work with me. I finished the stage ten minutes behind the winner. Do not be afraid to work with the race leader if it will benefit you and/or your team.

Note how the top continental riders in the Tour de France often choose one stage to make their victory bid.

Stage racing is so hard that there are very few riders who have the strength to make two or three bids. Once you have gained leadership you must have the strength left to defend it.

Most riders cannot afford – and the wise ones do not spend energy on long lone or weak breakaways – trying to bridge large gaps without sufficient help or by chasing every breakaway.

A puncture or mechanical breakdown in a long single stage or multistage race can result in loss of vital minutes. If you have no team car, or if it is not around when required and one of your leading rider's tyres puncture or they have mechanical trouble, someone in the team should either give him a wheel or a bike.

The Spanish team in the Tour of Britain used excellent strategy to return a teammate 'off the back' with trouble, to the bunch, with minimum effort. When one of the riders had trouble and stopped, his teammates carried on riding with the bunch, then about every 400 yards a Spaniard would drop back from the bunch and stop. When the trouble was rectified, the first Spaniard would re-mount and ride flat-out for 400 yards, where the second teammate (already moving) would make a similar effort to the third teammate; with each rider doing just his 400 yards and then sheltering behind the fresh teammate until the group rejoined the bunch.

Should one of the lower placed teammates stop with trouble, the others should try and slow the bunch down. After four minutes or so look back down the road and if you can see that your teammate is struggling in the distance to get back in the race again, two of you should drop back and help him over the last few hundred yards when his effort is faltering.

When you have eight riders in your team, all of them must not stop if a rider has trouble. Split your team in two. Four riders should drop back, one at a time.

PREPARING TO RIDE IN A STAGE RACE

The other four should slow down the bunch. After a few miles, look back down the road and if your teammates are in sight, drop back and help them over the final stretch. This technique prevents the whole team being left by a speedy bunch when 'off the back' helping a rider in trouble. Change these groups as the race progresses, swapping your two top riders with three lower placed riders.

Felice Gimondi at the 1969 Giro dell'Appennino.

When there is a competent servicing crew following the race and you have trouble, calmly plan your actions. If you can ride on for a while, ask a team mate to drop back and tell the servicing man about your trouble while you sprint ahead of the bunch. Should the fault be in your rear wheel, change to the small sprocket and release your brake ready for a quick wheel removal.

When the servicing team arrive, do not panic – keep out of their way and let them get on with their job. As soon as they have finished, select your correct gear, get on your machine and let the mechanic hold your machine while you fasten your feet in. Do not jump on your cycle and flounder away in too high a gear struggling to get your feet in the clips.

DEFENDING RACE LEADERSHIP

The best time to make a definite bid to gain race leadership is later in the race when the field is more strung out (on general classification) and the danger men have shown their form. You and your team can pick out three or four danger men and concentrate on them mostly, keeping half an eye on any good outsiders.

Remember it is far harder to gain race leadership once you've already had it; everyone knows you are in form and will be watching you. Far better to save yourself until later in the race and try to catch the leaders off guard, even if this means missing out on some of the glory (like a stage win early in the race which would give you race leadership).

Once you gain and decide to defend race leadership, you must pick out one or two dangerous rivals, and watch them and them alone. The rest of your team must take on the next three or four danger men and help you bridge the gap to any dangerous breakaways. You will only exhaust yourself and your teammates if you attempt to catch every breakaway. There is always someone in the bunch concerned with riders in the breakaways. A rider in the bunch, lying 10th on general classification, will worry about riders in 11th and 12th positions on general classification in the breakaway, but if these riders see the race leader and his team are bringing back all the breakaways they will often not help him. Finally, when you and your team are exhausted by these 'wild goose' chases, a 'danger' man who has been watching and resting in the bunch will attack you and you will be too tired to respond.

PREPARING TO RIDE IN A STAGE RACE

All your team must keep near the front of the bunch to be on hand for any attack. Space your team out near the front of the bunch, encouraging the leading riders, by example, to do a bit. Not many people attack when the pace is kept brisk, so it pays to keep the bunch moving.

In a stage race you must have a brain like a calculating machine. Every danger man and every potentially dangerous breakaway must be recognised instantly. A decision whether to chase must be instantaneous, for the longer you delay the wider the gap opens. Have your wits about you in every situation and see if you can take advantage of it.

In a classic stage race we had the race leader and another rider lying fourth. We were having a rough time defending the leader. A small breakaway of unimportant riders, on this particular stage, was half a minute in the lead and all the highly placed riders were trying to get through to join it. We were having our work cut out to prevent them and I could see our team were tiring under the pressure from these unceasing attacks. I dropped back and suggested to my teammate, lying in fourth, that when the next strong rider, who was down on general classification, attempted to bridge the gap, he should chase and pretend to try to slow him down. Once well clear of the bunch he should start to work with the rider and catch the breakaway.

Soon a strong rider, who had crashed and lost time earlier in the race, attacked and my teammate gave chase. No one in the bunch bothered until our rider suddenly started to work and then hell was let loose for the next fifteen minutes. Highly placed riders saw the danger and attacked and attacked, and we had to jump round like 'cats on a hot tin roof' to prevent anyone escaping. Our rider contacted the group and when we managed to slow down the bunch they disappeared out of sight.

Our team and race leader then had the easiest ride of the tour. We just sat sheltered and watched the danger men only while their teammates worked to stop the breakaway from getting too big a lead. I had dreams of our team having first and second on general classification, but unfortunately my dreams were shattered.

Firstly, our rider lying 8th on general classification punctured and two of us eased to help him back. An easy job, I thought, with the bunch riding so steadily. Was I wrong?

We chased and chased, dropping one teammate as we desperately fought to get back. When we finally made contact the whole field was strung out behind our yellow jerseyed, attacking teammate.

I finally fought my way to the front and asked him what on earth he was doing. He said lamely, his teammate in the breakaway was attacking him.

Round the next corner we caught the breakaway and stopped at a level crossing. Once again, we were under attack from the whole field. Our depleted team, now exhausted, could not respond and the breakaway pulled away without us.

At the finish our race leader hung on to a reduced lead. A new challenger was close behind to torment us for the remaining days.

So our race leader — by his thoughtlessness or selfishness — nearly lost us the team race, one teammate his 8th place and the other a chance of 1st or 2nd. Finally, he put his own position in jeopardy.

Always ride as a team; learn to trust and help each other. Remember to put yourself in your teammates' place, if he is away, or 'off the back', and consider how he will want you to assist him — tomorrow you may be in the same position.

In the Tour l'Avinia, the Italian race leader was under a strong attack from the Spanish top-class riders. Two of the Spaniards were two minutes in front of the 'main bunch' in a strong breakaway. One Italian, lowly placed on general classification, was also in the 'break', but his slowing tactics were having no effect. The Italian team manager called him to drop back to the bunch and meanwhile called the rest of his team to the head of the 'bunch'. Soon the complete Italian team were echeloned and doing a fast team pursuit at the front. No other rider was allowed in to help or hinder. After twenty miles of this flat-out effort, with the rest of the field strung out in a long thin broken line behind them, they caught the Spaniards.

The England and/or Northern teams in the Tour of Britain should have copied this when yellow jersey-ed Pokorny (the Pole) broke away from the field and increased his lead on general classification, while the English teams back in the bunch were at sixes and sevens. In such a situation you must get organised — as the Italians did above — if you want your team to stand any chance in the race later on.

Cycle racing is the ultimate sport, and stage racing is the ultimate in cycle racing. Courage, fitness, comradeship, tactics and luck all play their part.

The struggles, stresses and elations of a lifetime of experience are seemingly crammed into a fortnight's stage racing.

CHAPTER 12

RACE ORGANISING

This is one of the most important and most neglected aspects of our sport. The only procedure laid down is usually how to pay your dues and how to inform the police and the British Cycling Federation of the details of the race. Every club, in addition to other small promotions, should try to run at least one classic race, to give the riders in the club a chance to ride against or watch some of the country's top riders. Top riders should give spectators in the area something worth watching, attracting more support and perhaps young spectators who may be inspired and join the club. The club will then have helped to provide good racing and will have benefited the riders who are down for international selection.

Your first consideration when trying to promote a classic race must be to gain and keep the interest of the spectators. The reasons for this are:

1 Sponsors are more interested in sponsoring events which attract large crowds, and this will ease your financial difficulties.

2 It encourages riders (nothing is more demoralising than winning a classic race with only twenty spectators watching).

3 How grand would it be to be able to promote cycling to the position of National Summer Sport? Surely we could beat cricket in terms of excitement. But we must show, and show regularly, our sport in its best light, to succeed. Cyclists say, 'Why don't they televise cycling?' Would you, if you were a Television Chief, when only a small proportion of the public are interested enough to turn out to watch the event live?

Try to position your course as near to largely populated areas as you can manage. Mohammed must go to the mountain!

Find a small circuit, about two to seven miles round, preferably in a park, promenade, private grounds or round a factory if the surface is reasonable, and over eight feet wide. If you can, get your promotion to fit in with a local carnival. Any club near a seaside resort should not hesitate to solicit the council's help by bringing to its notice the races at other seaside towns. New spectators cannot be expected to wait half an hour between laps; so if you have to, use the highway and see whether the police will allow you to use a small circuit.

If the police insist on the 10-mile lap, run two events simultaneously to keep the public interested and/or try to get the army territorials (or yourselves) to fix a walkie-talkie tie up with various parts of the course, to relay what is happening.

When the race is over 60 miles, then an interesting variation is, if possible, to make the riders complete one large circuit of, say, 40 to 60 miles before coming on to complete several laps of a small final circuit. Any dropped rider who arrives after the leaders could either be disqualified or issued with a coloured band to show he is a lap behind. On the Continent many multi and single-stage races finish with two or three laps in or near each end of the stage town. This is a very good idea and gives the spectators something more of the race to watch than merely the bunch flying down the last 200 yards of road. I consider it a good policy for our races to follow.

Before writing to big establishments, approach personally, if possible, any factories, shops, wholesalers and the local council in your area and tell them what you are doing about the sport. Show them another good programme, especially if it contains advertisements by similar types of firms and explain how it will benefit them far more than the everyday type of advertisement. We charge £5 for a full-page advertisement, £3 for a half-page and IOS. for a quarter-page in our programme.

Should you get a great deal of support, take over a full page in the local paper. Most papers will let you have the centre free if you and your advertisers will pay for the rest. On the other hand, if you cannot gain support, but you have an ideal course, run a raffle or jumble sale to get the money.

Search round until you find a good but cheap printer. For 1,000 programmes we have been charged from down to £30 including posters, so you can see that it is well worth the effort. The sooner you can do all this the better; but spread the work out by getting other members of the club to help. Design your posters carefully and dramatically, make them as big as possible, and get as many as you can afford since they are not expensive. Stickers facing inwards on local buses are a good idea. Have the posters put up round the town by a hoarding firm. Visit shops and hotels near the course and enquire if the smaller posters can be placed in the windows. Perhaps the occupants will sell a few programmes for you. If you are very keen, try selling extra programmes in public houses near the course on the Saturday evening before the race. Sometimes advertisements round the posters provide a little extra income. Print a map on your posters and programmes if possible; this attracts and helps the public to follow the route better. Order your loudspeakers, usually one stationary and one mobile (cheaper on your own car) and again shop for the cheapest (but ensure they are efficient).

Well in advance obtain police approval of the course you require if it is on the open road.

Ask the St. John ambulance men or women to attend.

About two months before the event everything should be ready or ordered, and you should have some idea of your minimum prize list. Send round the circular containing race details and total prize money to all the leading clubs and teams, inviting entries. To have the event in the B.C.F. handbook helps in this respect. Send more invitations to local clubs than to those far away unless your event is exceptional. We usually send off about sixty invitations.

Have a meeting on the day after the race closing date to select the field and send back any excess entries without delay so that the riders can enter another race.

Race organisers should only accept entries of the best riders in an oversubscribed, unless the rider's clubs do not promote any sufficient races (if so the riders must be told why they were rejected).

Get at least two people to practice some interesting commentary ready for the loudspeakers, as nothing is more annoying to the spectators than long crackling silences. Some music to play helps to give the commentators a rest. Arrange to have press coverage or ask the club press-secretary to do a write-up and dispatch it to the press on race day.

In the programme, carefully arrange the prize list. £15 to £20 is ample for first prize. Spread the prizes well down the finishing list. Have plenty of primes and/or points prizes to liven up the racing.

Most good riders spend about £150 to £200 each year to enable them to race. Very, very few will win half of this back.

Do not charge for programmes, ask your distributor to ask for a donation – you will get far more.

Try to arrange a free programme lottery. We permutated two riders numbers and any person holding the programme with the riders' numbers who finish first and second in the correct order wins a good prize. This gives spectators an extra reason to cheer their riders on.

KING OF SPORTS

Give careful instructions to the competitors on how to get to the changing rooms from various directions.

Make known details of gradients and road surface so that riders know what gears to fit and what tyres to use.

Inform spectators where the best vantage points are and details of the best and local riders.

Include a write-up about the sport, tactics, your club and offer any new members three months' free membership.

Thank the police, St. Johns, advertisers, donators, helpers and anyone else who has contributed to the event.

Arrange on a large-scale map how you want the course marshalled and arrowed on race day. Six arrows on each corner, two on the left and two on the right at 20 and 10 yards before the bend and two opposite to the bend.

Two marshals should be named for each junction to keep each other company and to make doubly sure the bend is covered.

If you are short of members, ask other local clubs or the scouts to help out.

Have a van to go round with spare marshals just before the start to fill any gaps and make sure all the arrows and flags are in position.

Inform the marshals that they must not stand in the road, either waving traffic to stop, or the riders on. They are to guide, warn and observe the riders, making sure they are obeying the rules of the road.

Rope off the finishing straight and brief two big members to keep the spectators behind the ropes.

Have a marshal with a red flag 200 yards down the road from the finish to warn oncoming traffic when the finish is imminent.

Try to arrange a spares car and motorcycle, even if this means charging the competitors an extra 6d. entry fee for the petrol and perhaps asking them to provide spare wheels etc. I am sure riders would appreciate this. Nothing is more frustrating than to puncture early in a race after perhaps travelling a long distance to the event with the additional cost of an overnight stop.

Make sure your numbers are clear and clean. If you are running several events make the numbers follow on to avoid confusion: 1 to 50, 51 to 100 etc.

Try to get a star or a local personality or 'big-wig' to present the prizes somewhere near the finish, immediately after the race. This not only adds the crowning touch for rider and spectator but rounds the event off properly. Only give prizes to

RACE ORGANISING

the first three or so riders, otherwise it takes too long, and in any case it is difficult enough to get even three riders together at the finish. Make sure your finishing judges know exactly what they are doing. Split them up: two should note 1st and 2nd placed riders; another two for 3rd and 4th and two for 5th, 6th and 7th placed riders. I have often seen all the judges taking the first two and missing the rest.

Weekend, holiday stage races, or a series of evening races can easily be promoted by several adjacent clubs. Each club can organise one stage; obtain marshals and adverts for the programme and allot the awards for its stage, with the entry fees going towards general classification awards.

Any local donors who usually help clubs, could also contribute towards general classification awards.

When organising schoolboy or girl events, contact the area school sport's officer and try to enlist his support.

Unless the event is a time trial it must be on a closed circuit and for this type of event you need a separate course insurance from the B.C.F. (Note this applies to all closed circuits).

Send attractive posters and entry forms to all schools in your area.

Besides the usual entry form details, include these:

a) All riders must be aged between 13 and 16 years

b) All cycles must be clean, have no mudguards, have two good brakes, a free wheel and be mechanically sound

c) Riders must be smart, wear shoes and dark shorts

d) All riders' parents must sign agreeing to the indemnity clause (included on the entry forms).

Unless your entries are evenly matched you should make your event handicapped. If the event is ten miles, base your handicap on the following: one minute for every year under sixteen. One minute for each of the following if the riders answer 'No'—Have you toeclips? Have you cycling shoes? Have you ridden 80 miles? Have you ridden 20 miles? Have you raced before? Have you finished in the first ten in any race? Have you finished in the first three in any race?

KING OF SPORTS

The organiser and his team should draw up a list of race day duties so that nothing is forgotten and everyone from the Chief Judge to the Marshal on the final bend know exactly what is expected of them. If either fail, the race can be ruined.

RACE DAY DUTIES

ORGANISER

Get to the H.Q. one hour before the start. Ensure all Chief Officials arrive. Make sure everything is running smoothly. Be at the race finish line half an hour before finish. Thank all outside helpers and look after any visiting celebrities.

CHIEF JUDGE

Report to organiser at H.Q. one hour before start. Ensure that all prime judges are briefed and at their positions in good time with the correct flags. Follow the race in the 1st car with the B.C.F. commissaire. Keep riders disciplined. Arrive at the finish 15 minutes before the leading riders. Brief finishing Judges. Ensure 200 yards and finishing flags are in position. Mark finishing line. Make out full result sheet for organiser and keep a copy for yourself.

CHIEF STEWARD

Ensure that the H.Q. is open 1 1/4 hours before the race starts. Report to organiser when he arrives. Hand 'sign on' sheets numbers, pins and box for licences over to competitors stewards. See seats and benches are set out and litter bins are in position. Check that the machine examiner arrives on time and the riders know where he is. Give him some raffle tickets to give to the riders when their bikes have been passed. With twenty minutes until the start, allow reserves to sign on in order of preference.

Look after H.Q. whilst the race is in progress.

Have plenty of hot water and washing facilities ready for when the riders finish. Have tea and sandwiches ready for riders and officials. Ensure the H.Q. is left tidy when everyone has gone.

CHIEF MARSHAL

Report to organiser at H.Q. one hour before the race starts. Mark off on your list the marshals as you dispatch them. Give marshals on bad bends red flags. Fifteen minutes before the start go round the course with spare marshals. Check that all arrows are in position. Put 'One mile to go' post in position, rope off the finish and position finish marshals. Thank any police who are helping for their co-operation. Collect all flags and arrows at the completion of the race.

CHIEF MOBILE MARSHAL

Report to organiser at H.Q. 45 minutes before the start. Brief other mobile marshals and officials following car drivers.

Riding pillion on a motorcycle, keep the official convoy in order, warn off other following vehicles and signal other traffic when it is safe to overtake the bunch.

Inform the second spares vehicles to go ahead when the breakaway group of riders is 1 minute in front of the bunch.

Help the Chief Judge to maintain discipline; under his directions withdraw any riders guilty of misconduct.

Report to the Chief Judge any offences reported by stationary marshals or mobile marshals.

ASSISTANT ORGANISER

To assist the organiser and stand in for any of the chief officials who fail to arrive or are very busy.

COMPETITORS STEWARDS

Report to Chief Steward 45 minutes before race starts. Ensure all riders have had their machines examined before they sign on. Check that licences are correct and keep them as a deposit on the riders' number. If a rider forgets his licence, write to his division to check he has one and in the meantime take 5/- deposit for his race number. If all the chosen riders have not signed on half an hour before the event starts, allow reserves to ride. Help Chief Steward while the event is on. Sign riders off and return licences for race numbers. Help Chief Steward at completion to tidy event H.Q.

MACHINE EXAMINER

Take a few tools for minor adjustments. Report to Chief Steward one hour before race starts. Check that tyres are very secure, tread and walls are in reasonable shape, wheels are true, brakes are perfect, the gears will not go into the spokes and accessories are secure. Ensure cycles are clean. Issue each rider with a card or ticket when his machine has been found satisfactory.

Check cycles and wheels carried by spares vehicles.

1ST CAR DRIVER

To report to Chief Judge half an hour before race starts. Stay 25 yards minimum distance away from the tail end of the main bunch for most of the race. Passengers: Chief Judge, Commissaire and any V.I.P. guest.

2ND CAR DRIVER

As above. Stay 5 car lengths minimum behind car 1. Passengers: Assistant Judge and the Press. Take 1st Car position if this is vacated.

CAR 3 DRIVER (SERVICE VEHICLE)

As car one. Drive 5 lengths behind car two unless signalled by Chief Mobile Marshal to follow breakaway. Return to the behind bunch if the bunch closes to within half a minute of breakaway. Passengers: Mechanic and his assistant. Check that spares are carefully and securely stowed and accessible.

CAR 4 DRIVER (2ND SERVICE VEHICLE)

Same as car three. Take car 3's place when it goes ahead to follow a breakaway. Passengers: same as car 3 with another medical attendant.

All Judges to report to the Chief Judge, all Marshals to the Chief Marshal and

RACE ORGANISING

so on, for final briefing and to let them know you have arrived. Report 40 minutes before the race starts. Make sure you know exactly what you are doing before you leave the H.Q. on race day.

Above all, do not say you might turn up to help. Be definite, and if you say you will help, do so.

Even if for some reason your club cannot run a classic race, it should certainly manage at least three ordinary events. If you do, try to put a little extra into them, especially as regards the organisation, type of course and prize money. Our sport is so expensive that to win something back is a nice change and encouraging for every rider. Try to run races of varying contours in your region so that your riders have a chance to develop in both flat and hilly races. This should also ensure that one type of rider does not dominate every event.

Whether your event is a classic or a schoolboy's, make sure the organisation is always first class.

Every club should have a race organisers' kit kept in a locked cupboard, so that anyone organising a race in the club or section can hire or borrow the items they require for their event from the club storekeeper. The kit should consist of:

(a) Transistor loudspeaker made to fit quickly onto any car. Costs approximately £15

(b) Twin orange flashers on either side of a board on which is written CAUTION CYCLE RACE APPROACHING and this can speedily be adapted to fit any motorcycle or car. Cost—homemade—approximately £3.

(c) Flags—
One: Union Jack; black and white chequered; red and white chequered; yellow.
Two: White, blue and green.
Five: Red.
Cost – homemade – approximately £3.

(d) Alloy boards measuring 8 x 16 inches, background painted day glow red with black markings; fifteen arrows, four 'DANGER' signs, three 'STOP' signs; two 'ONE MILE TO FINISH' '1/2 MILE TO FINISH' signs; 3 'TO CHANGING ROOM' signs. These signs are all fastened to 4 ft. 6 ins. stakes. Cost – home made – approximately £3 IOS.

(e) Riders' numbers. Make sure they are clean and clear. Plastic ones are the best. Box of large safety pins.

(f) Two long ropes and 30 stakes to rope off finishes.

The loudspeaker enables the Chief Judge and Announcer in the first official car to keep the riders in order and the spectators informed.

A motorcycle should be 400 yards in front of the bunch with the flashers on to warn any day-dreaming motorists of the approaching race.

The flags, direction, warning and distance signs make sure the riders are in no doubt as to what is ahead.

The kit helps to ensure a smooth-running, well-disciplined event. This good for riders, organisers and the police. Every Division and enterprising club should have at least one complete kit.

These are some notes I made out as a guide for our sponsored Leyland Grand Prix. This classic costs about £180 to run, £100 is provided by our main sponsor.

RACE ORGANISING COMMITTEES' NOTES

Some months before race
Try to obtain a main sponsor (see if someone in the club knows someone on the board of a big company etc.).
See local council for support.
Find a suitable course.
Ask police if course is suitable if its on the highway.
Put race in B.C.F. handbook and inform your division racing secretary.
Try to arrange a continental team.
Put race in local and national 'What's on' booklets.
Ask local newspapers for support.

Four months before race
Find and contact a celebrity to present the prizes, ask them to arrive half an hour before the finish.
Arrange for a good commentator and service vehicles.

RACE ORGANISING

Try to arrange T.V. and Radio coverage.
Contact St. Johns for first aid and the army for walkie-talkie hook up.
Get quotations from printers for programmes and radio shops for loudspeakers.
Find suitable changing rooms.
Contact police to put 'no parking' signs at the finish, and for two special constables to do crowd control.
Arrange for stands, seats, ropes and barriers for the finish and the judges' platform.
Contact local businesses for adverts.
Arrange for car park near the finish – half goes towards car fees for the land-owner, half for club.
See if band or group can play at finishing area.

Two months before the race
Send out race entry forms, ask for riders' personal details for commentators.
Write to newspapers, magazines etc., ask them to send correspondents.
Arrange following cars and drivers, and motorcycles.
Paint direction boards detailing corners etc., as in Isle of Man Races but smaller.
Arrange for refreshment bar and attendants for spectators at finish.
Make out course maps and detail people and their jobs.
Start to arrange programme and poster layouts (large size posters for following cars, to be pasted along their sides).
Ask local scouts for help.
Contact a good photographer and show him what is required.

One month before
Organise Trophy, replica, prize winners' vouchers.
Arrange for laurels and flowers for the winner, attending celebrity and sponsors etc.
Send T.V. people instructions if they are coming.
Programme printing etc. and competitors' instruction sheet.
Arrange accommodation for riders.
Find a suitable place and book meals for celebrity etc.
Have someone to look after foreign team.
Ask the club press secretary to look after the press: brief them during the race and arrange them transport. Furnish them quickly with the result.
Telephone other papers, radio etc., with a brief report.

KING OF SPORTS

Two weeks before race day
Send programmes to riders, police (via division) and advertisers etc.
Distribute posters and some programmes.
Give all officials, marshals, helpers, instruction cards stating what is required of them. Organise the tidying up after the finish.
Send Army, St. Johns, commentators, celebrities, V.I.P.'s guests, etc., final arrangements, telling them who to contact, where to contact them and who will look after them. Enclose programmes.
Check flags, numbers, pins, finish banner etc., are all available.

One week before the race
Send out pre-race write ups to T.V., radio, papers, etc.
Make out riders' sign-on sheet.
Make out Prime judges and finishing judges placing cards.

Day before the race
Tour round the race-course and local estates and shopping areas (about twice) with a loudspeaker car, briefly announcing the main attractions and distributing leaflets (a copy of the programme's front page).
Go round cafes, clubs and pubs in the evening giving leaflets and programmes out.

After the race
Send out the results quickly.
Write a letter of thanks to all concerned with the race.

CHAPTER 13
CYCLING CLUBS

I have often said that our ideas when it comes to clubs are wrong. We have far too many of them and most are not ambitious enough. Each club here has one or two good riders, but in France, once a rider shows any promise, he joins a big regional club where he is under the guidance of a trainer and where he trains with riders of his own class. Many towns here have two or three clubs, many with under ten active riders. This is not enough members to keep the whole operation organised. Too often they just rely on other clubs to promote events. There is also a strong tendency for these small clubs to persuade inexperienced riders to join them when they are not equipped to look after them. After burning them off in a couple of runs, they leave them disillusioned and ready to leave the sport.

I am not saying, by any means, that the big clubs we have do better but they have the manpower and could, with a little effort, get the capital and initiative required to continue their work. Just to illustrate what can be done: my club, with the help of no main sponsors, promoted seven 3rd and Junior road races and two classic races in one year. In the Junior events no less than £10 was offered in prizes, and a total of over £120 was spent in the promotion of the two classics. In four years we increased our membership from seven to over sixty active members.

How many races should your club promote? If you have only one team of three riders competing, then theoretically you should promote at least two events per year. If there are nine riders (three teams) you should promote at least six races, and so on. When your riders keep getting entries back because events are full then see if you can put on some more events. Encourage other clubs in your area to do the same.

I have known disappointed riders leave a big club because only one team from this club was being accepted for races. These riders form another club in the hope of being able to race frequently. Then the inevitable happens, the big club is weakened and the small club is not strong enough to promote events. This is bad for both. The only answer is for big clubs to promote more races and to have more teams accepted for events.

To run an efficient club which does not lean too heavily on one or two members, you should have a minimum of about fifty members of all ages and both sexes. I have explained earlier why a big club is better for racing, and the same argument applies for most of a club's social activities. When there are three or four clubs in your town with only small memberships try and get one or more of them to amalgamate into yours. Your club should cater for all types of cycling and cyclists: track, time trialists, road racing, cycle cross, rough trackers, tourists, schoolboys, veterans, etc. The more the merrier. What a grand cross section of exploits could be recounted by such a group in the clubroom. Cycling has enough outside adversaries without there being internal friction.

All ages and both sexes should be welcome. A club with members missing from either end of the age scale is at a disadvantage. The younger end give the club new blood and vitality. They can learn what cycling is about from the older members. The older members can give advice, act in official capacities and keep themselves fit. They can, by mixing with the young, stay young at heart.

When your club has general meetings ensure that all sections and age groups are represented. Should anyone have a problem or a grouse, they are encouraged to come forward and air it in front of them. Don't give members any opportunities to feel 'they don't care about us'. The bigger a club, the bigger its committee should be, to make sure all are represented. Have sub-committees for all club work, socials, racing, fund raising etc. Allocate specific jobs to as many members as possible. Don't ask for a lot of volunteers to turn up for a job and then have half of them milling round with nothing to do. This treatment will dampen their enthusiasm.

When you are electing your main committee only choose people who have proved their worth. Any enthusiastic member, as yet untried, may be put on one of the smaller committees to prove their worth. If your club is one of the usual types and is short of volunteers, don't grumble at someone and then beg him to do the job again. In fact, don't grumble if you're either too lazy or incapable of doing it yourself. Even racing people can find time to take on a committee job; very few jobs like these take more than an hour a week if business is kept up to date.

A club is only a success when members learn to give and take. Don't grumble with a group of sympathisers in a corner. Put your complaints and your suggested remedy in front of the relevant committee and say your piece. If you are defeated, then accept the majority decision with good grace.

While most of the club's attention and funds must be directed to the majority's interests, do not forget the minorities – the racing girls and cycle cross riders – and give them all the help you can.

CYCLING CLUBS

To get money in the bank is a difficulty facing most clubs. Members' subscriptions should be realistic. It is no use begging and scraping to make ends meet when members are rolling up on £70 bikes or in cars. Collecting weekly subs is a difficult and time-wasting task. A better idea is to make senior members pay a quarterly sum.

Raffles are quite good if your members are enthusiastic, but it is too close to begging for many people to enjoying doing it. A favourite way is a jumble sale. There I think you not only make a tidy sum but you are doing two sets of people a good turn. You are taking from the don't wants and giving to those who want.

A raffle can be profitably run by several clubs cooperating. Ten clubs each giving £10, plus expenses, can offer a very attractive £100 prize list.

If you have a lot of members, a supporters' club with a weekly draw is a good idea. Give each member a yearly membership number. This number will go into the drum every week. Each member pays 2/- per month, 3d towards the prizes and 3d. to the club each week. See if local tradesmen will give you your weekly prizes at cost price.

Don't go to extremes, either by banking large amounts or spending all. Pump most of your money back into the club but keep a little back each year for a rainy day or for any big project like a new clubroom.

Before approaching any sponsors make sure that you can give them value for money, and that their contribution is worthwhile for all the extra trouble and worry they will cause.

The club's social side is very important and without it many good racing clubs flounder and disappear. The social committee, although doing most of the organising, should enroll the help of ordinary club members as much as possible. Don't, for instance, expect one person to do all the work at the club's annual dinner. Get eight or ten people and ask each one to organise one dance or one game. Print a programme so that everyone knows what they are doing and when. Don't ask people to organise dancing and games if all you want to do is sit drinking in a corner all night and are not prepared to join in.

Hot-pot suppers, film shows, lectures, discussions, games and competitions are functions that can be laid on by the Social Committee once or twice a month, to enliven the club nights.

Good club runs are something that should not be left to chance. They should be organised over a three-month period; never, if possible, travelling in the same direction on any one road twice. Cyclists' cafes are getting harder and harder to find; make sure your club's behaviour in them encourages them to stay open for cyclists.

Do not let novices join your club if you cannot cater for them. If you have no experienced riders who are willing to take the inexperienced out on runs, then do not encourage them to join. It is silly to leave them exhausted and disillusioned after their first ride. Rather encourage them to join the C.T.C. If the local C.T.C. is poor or non-existent then, if you wish to expand your club, you must provide facilities for these youngsters.

If you want to race, then race – do not turn club runs into races. Of course, the occasional prime or mile dash to the cafe is good fun; but the riders should quickly re-group, then most of the journey should be made at the pace of the slowest. A big club again is at an advantage here, because it can run enough groups to suit every rider's pace.

Autumn is a time of year I always enjoy with our club. We organise a different event for each Sunday. Events such as a sports day (slow cycle race, hill climb, free wheel contest etc.) a treasure hunt, a paper chase (the hares using chalk), a barbeque; club or inter-club games of touch rugby or baseball all work well.

If your club begins to fail to attract new members, it's on its way out. Don't wait until it's too late, but start a recruiting campaign at once. Some of these ideas could help. Ask local cycle dealers to donate when each sport's cycle is sold or keen youngsters are building a cycle. Make a leaflet giving details of your club, offering three months free membership. Place attractive posters advertising your club in cycle shops, sports shops, youth clubs, schools, and cafes. Ask local schools if you can lecture, give film shows or road safety instruction. Invite local schools through posters, the press and letters to the P.E. instructors, to compete in inter-school reliability trials, treasure hunts and races.

The club Press Secretary is an important person. He is responsible not only for encouraging new members, through his press reports, but for educating the general public in cycling matters. See if, besides your weekly news columns, you can get a decent article in local papers once a month about some aspect of cycling. Another idea is to run a picture series on cycle racing, as many papers do on golf and cricket.

If your club does most of these things, then you can be proud. If not, then set about the challenging task now. Never join a club with the idea of getting something out of it – you will be continually disappointed. Join to put something in and the returns will be many. There are too many Jacks these days. Turn them out of your club if they continually unsettle it.

CYCLING CLUBS

When you decide not to race again do not sell your cycle for a quarter of its value and close the door on your sport. Try to put something back into the sport you have taken so much from. It doesn't need to take up much of your time. Our sport desperately needs experienced people in official capacities. Time-trial clubs always seem to have plenty of old stalwarts who turn up before dawn to help with events. Road Racing ex-riders could do with the same spirit.

When you have been racing since early season, finish racing before September and help to organise a late race, a couple of tourists or social events. This will help to repay club members who have helped in the races you have competed in.

I have stayed keen many years because I never make my season so long that I am fed up with it by the end. I am always ready and eager to start each January.

DIVISIONS

The divisional committee is chosen in a similar way to the clubs. Again, choose people of proved value. Divisions are often out of touch with what the racing men really want. If the committee is made up of non-racing men (racing men usually cannot spare the time to attend a meeting a long way from home) then have an advisory committee of the best racing men in your region. This enables the committee to keep abreast of the racing situation.

Divisions should encourage clubs under their control to team up when it comes to the following: fielding strong division teams in classic races (this enables your best riders to compete against the stars and learn how to ride with good team-mates); spreading divisions' events out to cover the season; ensuring all the riders who want to race are not having entries returned through lack of events (if they are, quickly organise your clubs to promote more races); promoting stage and evening events; obtaining one or two efficient organisers' kits to hire out to your clubs who lack them.

The continentals gain most of their power and speed by regular hard racing rather than by just regular training. Divisions should ensure their riders have the same opportunity.

I laugh when people criticise our amateur riders in the continental classics for their poor performances. How can we expect our under raced, full time working lads to compete with regular racing, part time European riders?

KING OF SPORTS

Each division or town should have a mid-week evening race at least once a week, throughout the summer. These events should be flat or undulating and about 25 to 35 miles long. To make the races flat out and to give the lower categories a chance, make most of these events handicap races.

Divisions should encourage their clubs to expand, perhaps by awarding a prize to the club with the largest percentage increase in membership each year.

The government has been promising more cash for sport for some time. We are still waiting!

Our government gave our richest sport more money to promote the World Cup. The rich get richer, and the poor get poorer.

Many organisations are already armed with schemes of what they will do with the government grant when it arrives. Ensure you are represented in your area. The Central Council for Physical Recreation (C.C.P.R.) is working on the idea, along with the A.A.A. and other bodies of large indoor and outdoor stadiums. Make sure you the needs of the sporting cyclist are represented.

Cycle tracks (particularly indoor) of the right size and shape must be called for and perhaps a road circuit round the sports field.

How grand it would be if our riders could train on an indoor track on dangerous icy and dark winter evenings. How safe for our schoolboys and junior riders to be able to train and race on a closed circuit.

The idea of each town having one central sports stadium and ground is an excellent one. The main indoor arena has a large centre playing area for five-a-side football, netball and basketball. Around this would be a running and cycle track. Adjoining buildings would be for swimming pools, gymnasiums, weight training, judo, boxing, children's play-rooms, coffee bar, lounge, etc.

Under one roof families, couples, youths or working groups could meet. They could have a good training period at their chosen sport, a shower, change and meet in the lounge afterwards.

Such a building and its surrounding playing fields could be used by schools during the day. The councils could centralise their staff and facilities. It is a waste of money to have the above sports dispersed all over a town each with separate ground staffs, night watchmen, caretakers, instructors, changing rooms and showers.

Contact your local education authority for use of one of the new, smaller indoor sports centres which are being built in most areas.

CYCLING CLUBS

Encourage schools in your area to put cycling on the school athletics curriculum. See if you can arrange for your local champions and coach to lecture and present cycling awards at keen schools. Take over a large local cinema once or twice a year and show good cycling films, and invite an international rider and top coach to lecture afterwards. To attract local youth, organise a sports forum with two or three popular sports. Each celebrity could speak, demonstrate and answer questions in turn. Offer each school and youth club a block of seats.

Make sure the local press in your area is never short of cycling news. See (do not write) the local sports editor and arrange for at least a couple of columns once a week.

When judging riders for offences try to be sensible as well as just. Go easy with the suspension ruling. To suspend a rider who has trained 16 hours a week for several months, for a month, will not only punish him for that period but can ruin his prospects for the rest of the season. To penalize a rider ten minutes into a stage race will ruin his chances completely. Such a penalty should be given only for a serious offence, especially when one thinks of the training, dedication and expense put in by a rider when they're competing in a big event.

The commissaire is the first line of discipline; 'little and often' should be the maxim. This is better than letting riders get away with offences, then suddenly jumping back in and knocking one unfortunate rider for six.

Here is what I believe is a reasonable guide for first offenders: double the penalty for their second offence. For switching; just clipping double white lines; not stopping dead at halt signs; litter dropping – one warning should be given, then disqualification from the race or a £1 fine or 1 minute penalty. For dangerous riding; using bad language; knowingly entering two events on the same day; causing inconvenience to other road users – suspension for two weeks or £1 10s fine or 2 minutes penalty. For jumping halt signs or lights at red; being a danger to other road users; causing other riders to crash – one month's suspension or 5 minutes penalty or £5 fine (or a combination of the two).

Fining is often the fairest way to give a five minutes' penalty to two riders for an offence in a stage race when one rider was leading the race and the other was an hour down.

Billy Holmes once lost a chance of winning the Tour of Britain through a time penalty for dropping litter, which probably cost Holmes about £200 in prizes.

KING OF SPORTS
NATIONAL POLICY

I was sad when I saw the B.L.R.C. and the N.C.U. join together. Not because I was a staunch supporter of one and despised the other. I belonged to both. I was disappointed because it meant a lack of friendly rivalry. The one trying to outdo the other meant fast progress. How much have we improved since? In 1954 we had a Tour of Britain, several very well organised classics, two large and several smaller sponsored teams. How can we put the fire into our sport? Some of the things I have already said about promoting better events, encouraging promoters and interesting the public will all help a great deal. But I think also that the right attitude from club to national official would be a blessing.

I attended the last B.L.R.C. A.C.M. and two B.C.F. A.G.M.s and found them appalling. The last B.C.F. A.C.M. which I attended spent a full day trying to get through over one hundred resolutions, and out of these there were not twenty which made for any progress and advancement of the sport. Of those stout twenty many were voted out because of lack of foresight and lack of knowledge. Arguments about changing 'and' for 'but' in Clause 4, 'this' for 'that' in Clause 10, and so on and so on. Over half a valuable hour was spent on arguing about motor paced racing – how much motor paced racing do we see in this country?

A way to get around this farcical procedure would be to allow or request each division to have only two resolutions, which they consider beneficial to the sport, to be put on the agenda for the National A.C.M. Any other proposals could be put before the racing, publicity or financial committees for consideration.

Let's not be timid when it comes to trying new ideas for the advancement of our sport. Be prepared to give them a try for a year or so; if they don't have the desired effect, withdraw them.

Divisions who put forward exciting ideas could be given the go-ahead to use them in their division. If they proved successful, they could be applied nationally. My proposal to allow women to ride against men in handicap races would have been an ideal test case.

Every year there's is a fight between the same officials for power. Yet in my opinion no official should be voted for a second term of office unless they've really advanced the sport in their first term.

Once I was nominated for a Racing Committee, of which there are about eight members. I have raced for England, promoted several top classics, of international status and belonged to one of the few expanding clubs in the country. I thought these qualifications were sufficient, yet I did not get sufficient votes.

I could not complain. In fact I could not have volunteered myself if I had thought the B.C.F. was bulging with men who would volunteer themselves and were full of fight and new bright suggestions. This is not the case. Some people volunteer to boost the prestige of the club and region, some as a stepping-stone for a higher national job; only a few have ideas and the intention of progressing the sport.

When a man in your region says he would like to be this or that nationally, before you nominate him look at his record and, unless it is excellent, say 'NO'.

I think it would be a good idea at national B.C.F. elections for each candidate to have after their name a write-up of what they have done for their club, region and national team. This is preferable to being confronted merely with a list of names of people you have never heard of, from far away regions, with the subsequent tendency for Northern people to vote for Northerners, etc. This way everyone would know the capabilities of the men they were voting for and would stop guessing. Far too many decisions which affect our sport are mishandled by these out of touch high officials.

The agreement with the police and the Ministry of Transport which legalised road racing but imposed many restrictions was in my opinion badly handled. After all the money collected from racing members to help fight proposed restrictions harmful to the sport, I think we were let down on two major points:

a. The restrictions on racing through built up areas. On a Sunday our towns can brag the quietest roads; it is the country-side and seaside roads which are congested. One point worthy of note is that the police, before the regulations came into force, asked our section not to race through a local beauty spot where the traffic was heavy on a Sunday. We obliged, and now, of course, we have every legal right to use this road. Yet the town through which we ran our Grand Prix of Preston is deserted on a Sunday. This was the town where we worked up interest in our sport. Our last event before the regulations had 9,000 spectators and attracted many new members from the area. Racing through towns was a great way of letting a large number of people see our sport.

b. the limiting of laps to over 10 miles. This was disastrous to our efforts to attract spectators, and again I can see no apparent, road-safety reason for this. A small circuit that does not cross major roads can easily be found. On a small circuit the riders must turn every few miles, preventing any build up to traffic behind the bunch. This can happen when the bunch follow a narrow or busy road for a long period of time.

More recently, the M.O.T. introduced 40 m.p.h. limit roads. We of course backed down and agreed to accept these as the 30 m.p.h. racing restrictions. How ridiculous! Let the deadly car speed up but keep the racing cyclist out, say the police. We agree!

I think the B.C.F. should now make every effort to meet the Ministry of Transport and the police with the intention of getting these bad decisions reversed.

I believe the Racing Committee should be vigilant and, whenever a club or division reports that the police are exerting any pressure to curb road racing, they should arrange a meeting between the Racing Secretary B.C.F., Racing Secretary of the division concerned, and the Chief Constable of the area. These meetings would prove to the police that they are not just fighting an individual organiser but the whole of the B.C.F. They would enable us to come to a better understanding with the police.

The choosing of riders for international events seems to be done by black magic. Riders seem to be chosen either the year after their peak or just because they are usually chosen and once rode well abroad. In the I.O.M. internationals, how often is it announced just before the start that there are one or two changes in the Continental teams? I have noticed that these men often win. This, in my opinion, is because right up to the last minute, Continental managers will find a place for a man currently in form – a policy we should follow. Riders are also chosen for the wrong events: climbers for flat races; stage riders for single-stage races and so on.

To assist international riders, the B.C.F. should write to their employers asking them to give the rider time off work to compete. Many of our riders have been sacked for having time off to race abroad. I feel that this might have been avoided had the managing directors of the firms concerned received a personal letter from a high official in the B.C.F., pointing out the honour and national prestige attached to a rider being selected to ride for his country. If it's possible to have the rider's firm mentioned in the programme and press reports, this would help a great deal.

As I suggested in the Divisions, penalties on riders and officials should fit the crimes. To drop a rider from a national team because he missed an official dinner is ridiculous. Professionals and independents who wish to revert to amateur cycling after a couple of years of being retired should be encouraged to do so. We vitally need these experienced riders to stay in the sport. They could, of course, have a limit on their prizes, and would not be allowed to compete internationally.

CYCLING CLUBS

The B.C.F. should, with all haste, form an efficient and enthusiastic publicity and projects committee. The first job of the committee would be to help and encourage clubs and divisions to obtain more space in the local newspapers. They must visit editors of the large daily papers and try to persuade them to give more coverage; including photographs, information on the number of cycles sold each year and explaining how many millions of cyclists there are.

Some cycling reporters have no idea how to report cycle road racing and road racing tactics, and they should be educated in this. I have been a race leader and a member of the winning team in several major events covered by the cycling magazines and the daily press, yet I have never been interviewed to give the story on the tactics or personal anecdotes from the race. They flash past the riders a couple of times in the event, take a picture of the winner and think that is all there is to it. No wonder the man in the street looks dubious when you mention cycle race tactics. I wonder how many reporters know of their existence.

Perhaps Rene De Latour with his personal stories of riders could give some much-needed advice. You never read of riders being criticised for bad tactics or bad team support or praised for a good tactical maneouvre; this is probably because some reporters don't have the knowhow.

It is high time the British Public and government were made to realise the fanatical appreciation of the sport abroad and its potential for national prestige. 100,000 spectators watched the finish of the Peace Race. Factory workers are given time off to watch the Tour of Spain. The Italian government is involved in squabbles over team selections. The fact that most British riders train in their spare time is of no interest. Only the winners are noticed and extolled. We should give our athletes and riders full opportunities and facilities or not bother sending them at all.

This committee would also approach the television chiefs annually and ask for at least eight events to be televised for 15 minutes per event. I fail to see how, if a sensible argument were put forward, they could refuse to give cycling a quarter of an hour or so coverage per month when other sports have at least a couple of hours per week.

The committee would ensure the events chosen attracted large crowds, were on an interesting course and had top class riders. Perhaps a few continental classics could be included.

I suggest that we ask the television people to film the whole event, and in the studios to cut down the film to show the exciting parts. A good four-hour race should provide an action-packed 10 to 15 minute presentation. This way an amateur promoted event can be given a professional recording. The only good way to get close-ups is from the pillion of a motor-cycle or using tele-photo lenses or, better still, several cameras combined. If possible, show the cameramen a Continental racing film so we don't get the present type of fleeting shots shown on current T.V. sports flashes. We do not wish to lose public and T.V. interest because of poor filming.

This committee should approach as many large companies as possible, both cycling and non-cycling, to try to persuade them to sponsor either a race or racing team. The argument about good advertising, tax relief and aiding a good young sport ought to help. The Communist countries are always trying to prove themselves superior, and the use of sport here would be a chance for our private enterprise companies to try to prove otherwise by helping our sport.

Every effort should be made to encourage our large cycle and cycle accessory firms to give a hand. We have some of the largest in the world, yet their contribution to the sport must rank with the smallest in other countries. It distresses me to see them copying the lines of modern road racing cycles, having contributed little or nothing to the sport that evolved them.

The committee would have to watch out for any of our present sponsors withdrawing their support, and if it learns that this is liable to happen, to make all haste to iron out any trouble. When the company in question will not continue, the committee should make note of their complaints and try to make sure that it does not happen with other sponsors.

If a club which has been organising races for a sponsor finds, for some reason, that it cannot continue, then it must inform the B.C.F. as early as possible, so that another club can continue the event. An International race was nearly lost once, not because the sponsors (a City Corporation) wanted to withdraw, but because the promoting club were either too lazy or too under-staffed to organise the race.

The ideas this type of committee could investigate are, among others, to see if we could apply the Danish Tote System to road racing in this country, to run a sponsored series of seaside racing on a points championship system at the big seaside resorts; to run a national handicap race with handicap heats and organise a final at Crystal Palace.

The Tote System used in Denmark should be applied, for a trial period, on a couple of tracks and closed road circuits in this country as soon as possible.

CYCLING CLUBS

I am sure 50 to 100 cyclists in full cry could beat 6 dogs or 12 horses for excitement. The money obtained could be used to build indoor tracks, closed road circuits and all the amenities available to a prosperous sport.

We must make our racing faster and more attractive by having better courses and more prize money spread over more of the finishers.

Too many of our best riders pack in the game because it is too expensive; 90% of our racing riders are under 22 years of age. Our racing fields lack the experienced riders to pass on techniques to the younger ones.

One classic in the North and one in the South each week should be the aim with once a month or six weeks, a combined event taking place in the Midlands. This would reduce the expense of riders seeking international representation and would simplify the selectors' job.

The dates of all races should be fixed by the B.C.F. unless the race is part of a carnival or similar date fixed event to prevent the present clashing of fixtures.

Classic status of events should be reviewed every year so that events which drop in quality can be replaced by up-and-coming enthusiastic promotions. Leading riders should vote for an 'Event of the Year'; considering the size of the crowd watching, prizes, organisation, course, road safety control and changing rooms in that order.

Once we get an interested public our sport will begin to prosper. I think that first prize of at least £20 and a plaque should be given by the B.C.F. to the winning promoter, encouraging these essential and vital members of our sport.

CHAPTER 14
THE MANUFACTURERS

The attitude of the majority of cycle manufacturers seems to be 'sell 'em, forget 'em'. They don't seem to realise that one keen cyclist inspires interest in others, and that a satisfied customer will return. They seem to think that if the novice can stay upright on a moving cycle, that is all he needs to obtain full benefit from his new machine.

I nearly abandoned my first ride because my saddle was set too high. Luckily, I met an old club rider who saw my plight and rectified the fault for me. Many people I know when they bought a new cycle, having heard of clubs covering over a hundred miles, tried to emulate them; worn out, saddle sore, and disillusioned they decided that cycling was not for them.

A pamphlet should be given with every cycle sold.

Firstly it should cover road safety for the cyclist. Cyclists don't have to pass a driving test; most don't even have an elementary knowledge of the Highway Code.

Secondly it should show the new owner a comfortable basic position, and how to obtain it.

Thirdly it should instruct the new owner how to obtain the best use of his gear; nearly all utility cyclists over-gear, thinking that a cycle, like a car, should stay mostly in top gear.

Fourthly it should detail basic servicing, adjustment and replacement of components. Car manufacturers do it with a far more complicated piece of machinery.

Fifthly if the cycle is a sports model, advice should be given about joining a cycle club, undertaking moderate initial rides, how to get fitness, enjoyment and satisfaction out of cycling.

If manufacturers acted upon this advice, more cycles would be sold to people for the enjoyment of cycling. One enthusiast spends more on his cycle than five utility riders.

THE MANUFACTURERS

We rely on copying out-of-date continental equipment. Many accessories are made with unusual threads and nut sizes, inaccessible screws, saddle pillars and handlebar stems having different diameters. Bottom brackets, wheel and pedal spindles are very difficult to adjust accurately. Bolts and nuts are not made out of high tensile steel; they strip and sheer on the least pretext.

Most nuts are not self-locking like those used in the aircraft industry and they vibrate off without the excuse of the old cobbles. Spoke nipples become round if a spoke key looks at them.

The flats on cones on wheels and pedals disappear or are too narrow. Bearing surfaces cannot be cleaned easily; oiling points require half a can of oil to ensure the bearing is fed. Bearings are rarely protected from dirt and moisture.

Lights are a matter of life and death to the cyclist; most are badly designed. Bulbs are held in place by a piece of bent tin. The front of battery lamps are usually crudely threaded, and to change a bulb on a dark, wet night becomes an ordeal. Lamps are poorly secured and bounce off into the road after the slightest bump. Rear lights are worse.

Tyres are often poorly-designed; the canvas is too weak, the treads too wide and shallow and are not properly matured. New brake-blocks rarely slide easily into the shoes. Gear cable nipples all differ and have to be filed or cut to fit snugly into the lever. One roll of tape is never sufficient to cover the handlebars. Headsets are a particular bind since they're difficult to adjust or replace, and they often work loose.

Bottom brackets are badly designed. The special spanners easily slip or will not fit when the crank is fitted, and their leverage is insufficient for the tightness required. Two long, tough spanners fitting on good gripping surfaces should fit on together so that the cone can be held at its correct setting while the locknut is rammed home tight.

How many of our cycle and accessory designers roll up to work in a car every day and have never ridden a cycle for years. Have the industries got a design and research centre?

What I have said earlier about helping the sport applies here. Some firms, I know, do a great deal; others, not enough. I would like to see more trade teams, a couple of coaching centres (one near Oxford and one near Harrogate would be ideal). A British hostel in France for riders to be accommodated at a reasonable fee, plus a percentage of their winnings. Riders, while away, taught to speak French. A British sponsored team abroad and active co-operation in running our sport.

The small-wheeled machines are a great triumph for British manufacturers. Many of them incorporated excellent quick release devises that would do a racing machine proud. I hope the search for something new, instigated by these machines, does not stop but inspires by its success our industries to lead the way in all forms of cycle and cycle accessory manufacture.

Beryl Burton OBE competing on the track in 1967 at the World Cycling Championships. That same year she set a new 12-hour time trial record of 277.25 miles – a mark that surpassed the men's record of the time by 0.73 miles and was not superseded by a man until 1969.

CHAPTER 15
COMRADES

PROFESSIONALS

This band of riders is one of the outcasts of British cycle racing – why, I do not know. Their sponsors are few; the press gives them little encouragement. Many everyday riders think of them as a poor version of the Continental professional.

It seemed ridiculous for Britain to have a professional class of riders until we had at least 200 active independents. Now we cannot fully support 60 professionals.

Here I would like to give you my opinion of the Professionals, what they have done for our sport and what could be done to help them.

Without the independent class of rider, we have lost to amateur races a large number of our most experienced and able riders. Many of them had wives and families and were unable to afford the high expense of competing in classic races all over the country. Have you noticed how few top amateurs stay with us for very long and how even fewer of them are supported by able teams

Most of the independents had knowledge gained by years of racing both here and abroad.

The independents were partly to blame for their initial downfall, although at the time they probably did not realise what was happening, but they should make sure that it never happens again. This was when one of our big manufacturers looked in at the then fast up-and-coming independents getting excellent publicity from the Press, especially from the Daily Express, and decided it was too good to miss. Instead of entering the sport quietly and getting new riders, they entered with a fanfare and signed up nearly every good rider from other concerns. These riders proceeded to be highly placed in every event, thus discouraging and causing actual abandonment of many trade teams who had encouraged and fostered the growth of the independent over the hard years previously. After throwing money here and there the manufacturers found they had spent a small fortune and withdrew their aid, leaving a path of destruction and a broken independent movement.

The same mistake has happened since. To have one or two teams dominating the racing scene is detrimental to the sport; the interested public; the competitors; smaller sponsors and, because of this, the big sponsors.

Various suggestions have been put forward. No sponsor, for instance, should sign up per year more than two men who are already professionals and who must belong to separate teams, unless the sponsor is taking over riders of a team who have been abandoned by their previous sponsors. No sponsor should be allowed to have more than four men in one event, unless most of the other teams have more riders.

The sponsors themselves keep an eye on how the expenses of the team are going, and if they are too heavy, they should tell the riders and discuss with them how the expenses can be cut down, and then cut them down. They should not wait until the end of the year and then sack the team and pack in because of the high expense. When concerns like Viking Cycles can afford to sponsor for so long, larger firms should manage easily. I suggest that any new or intending sponsors might discuss the problems with old established trade team bosses before they join the sport.

My suggestion at a B.C.F. conference that firms other than cycle manufacturers should be allowed to be sole sponsors, lost by a small majority. The opposition's argument was that the U.C.I. did not allow this. The U.C.I. was not thinking of our poor sponsorship when it made these rules, but of Continental cycle firms, much smaller than any of ours, who have faithfully backed the sport for many years. If some large cycle companies would not help, then we should have looked elsewhere.

The independents first helped to make great the 'Daily Express' tours. They were the first to interest the Milk Marketing Board in sponsoring a Tour. The B.C.F. should do all in its power to encourage more professional teams and then to find a sponsor for a Professional Tour. The amateur race should then become the Circuit of Britain as it previously was.

The U.C.I. has pressed our sport into making a professional class. Once again, they are considering only the big cycling nations. On the continent the sponsored club has replaced many of the old independent teams. There an amateur can ride full time until he has the class to become a full professional. In England after a few years there are only about six sponsored clubs.

The continentals now have special amateur licence holders who can race against the pros. Surely these are like independents, so we are back to square one again. I think Britain should issue such a license.

Our professionals seem a long way off making the ten to twenty thousand pounds per year that the top continental pros manage. With improvement in race organisation, more trade co-operation and the interest of two or three big concerns outside cycling, the English professional could have a good living and increase in numbers.

COMRADES

VETERANS

When does an athlete reach his peak, when does he begin to fade?

I should say an athlete reaches a peak generally between 22 to 25 years. At the moment he begins to lose form at about 30 years of age.

This is one of the tragedies of a man's life. Why should a person only be able to attain physical perfection for only about one tenth of their life span?

The reasons are: lack of knowledge of the body and its untold reserves; the louts in the background constantly nagging them to retire; lack of competition and rivals of an older age group; staleness, after five to ten years of hard competition and dedication, makes many an athlete long to put their feet up.

The ratio of 20 years build up: 10 years peak: 40 years run down, as it is now, should be – 20 years build up: 20 years peak: 30 years gentle run down.

This extended period of vitality could be achieved by these counter measures to the above four points; a medical report and training schedule of men of the Cerutty calibre by medical advisors realising (as few do) the value of hard training to cure and forestall the diseases of old age. The general public and sports editors should stop encouraging athletes in sports – other than boxing and the like – to retire at the first defeat. Athletes should keep their seasons short and occasionally have six months rest so that they always retain a keen outlook.

I consider that the feat of a 35-year-old champion beating the world, *is of far more value and consequence* than a 15 year old prodigy doing the same.

How many people realise that many veteran athletes are now doing faster times than the champions did 20 years ago? Could you imagine a man, 20 years old now, beating the stars of today's records, in another 20 years? I do not think this will happen; I am sure it will.

I look with admiration at the Cerruttys, Van Steenbergens and, more locally, the Sox Spencers of this world. I compare these men with sound chests and supple muscles with many of the wheezing, pot-bellied 40 plus men I know.

To keep in condition in later life you need to do more than go for a daily walk or play golf. A person should eat properly and exert themselves at least three times a week to keep fit.

This will keep the lungs, heart, muscles and organs in good condition,

Most people think muscles deteriorate with age, but this is untrue; muscles, like the rest of the body, deteriorate mainly through lack of use.

KING OF SPORTS

When I see old people doddering about old folks' homes or slumped on a park bench, I am saddened. I am sure that with a better physical education they could be enjoying an active, healthy, more useful and enjoyable retirement.

I consider that many P.E. instructors in schools misappropriate some of their time. They should concentrate more on discussing with pupils correct dieting, yoga exercises and the importance of keeping fit after forty.

Many local authorities, misguidedly, have upper age limits on their sports centres.

So do all you can to encourage the 'veterans'. Do not keep saying, 'It's time you packed in and give the young lads a chance'. Older men and women need to keep fit as much, if not more, than the young.

The Grand Prix of Leyland 1969. Peter Ward (left) is wearing clipless pedals, while Peter Matthews (right) has toe clip pedals like most cyclists at the time.

COMRADES

The Championissimo, Fausto Coppi, at the 1953 Giro d'Italia.

CHAPTER 16
THE LEGEND IN ACTION

Coppi has had a hard stage the previous day and is comfortably in the lead on general classification. The team manager is determined he must rest and recuperate.

Ahead already at the start of the day's major climb is Jan Nolten. An Italian domestic is chasing, but soon he cracks. The Italian team manager calls to Bartali, who after a great effort, only closes 3 minutes of the fast increasing 4, which the fighting Nolten has put between himself and the bunch.

The Italian team car pulls alongside the bent, straining backs of the bunch and reluctantly the manager calls through the megaphone 'Coppi'. An immaculate, yellow-vested figure sitting relaxed with eagle eyes looking over the straining backs of the sweating rivals, immediately responds. Thrust, swerve, and he is on the outside, out of the saddle, a dance with a blacksmith's power in every stroke; one, two, three revs and he is clear away.

Down he sits and the chase is on. He catches Bartali on a steep corner, struggling round the shallower outer perimeter. Contemptuously Coppi changes UP, and cuts past effortlessly on the inside.

The scene is now the summit: coaches and cars parked everywhere, the roadside packed 15 deep. Eyes strain down the mountain to a point 2 kilometres below where the road disappears behind a rock. A newsreel camera man balanced on a rocky vantage point suddenly shouts as a figure rounds the corner. Slowly, tortuously, seemingly very over-geared. Nolten approaches. Only a kilometer to the prime when another figure flies round the corner, and the roar goes up 'Coppi'. The chant with every smooth revolution is 'Co-ppi', 'Co-ppi'! Faster, faster the tempo of the chant goes. 20 yards from the prime he freewheels past Hassenforder and crosses the line with his hand raised to the crowd who have been privileged to see the 'Legend in Action'.

THE YOUNG BOBET ARRIVES

Coppi is once again tour race leader and is out in front in a lone breakaway. Back in the bunch Coppi's only dangerous rival is the fast-improving Louison Bobet.

Bobet has tried many times to escape and give chase, but the ever-watchful Italian team box him in at every move. Tears fall from Bobet's eyes; he beats his fists onto his bars as he sees his chances of victory slipping. Ahead Bobet notices there is a road working blocking the righthand side of the road. The front riders are already thinning out and moving across to the left. Suddenly with an explosive effort Bobet jumps and accelerates down the righthand side of the excavations, catching the Italians off guard on the wrong side of the road. They finally get through to the front in time to see Bobet disappearing in the distance.

The French crowd lining the route are thrilled to see their compatriot having a crack at the campionissimo. Bobet, responding to their cheers, slams his gear into top and, during the 15 Kilometres chase, never sits on his saddle.

Yet it is the crowd who rob Bobet, the better sprinter, of possible victory. Coppi hears the cry of 'Bobet' running through the spectators. Although Louison is still half a kilometre behind him, Coppi immediately accelerates. On the line, he beats Bobet by a close margin.

BILL BATY

Bill Baty, the witty Tynesider has had my sides aching on many a pre-race evening with tales of the road. Here are a few I recall.

Warsaw – Berlin – Prague. Bill isn't doing too well. The terrible roads and daredevil riding of the continentals have shaken his confidence.

Bill notices that the only team to avoid the hurley-burly are the Czechs. Their manager has them doing a team time trial just behind the main bunch. At the halfway stage they sprint up to the bunch, straight through and away. Usually, they finish highly placed. Bill decides to join in with the Czechs.

The next stage starts, Bill drops back, and after a bit of pushing and shoving, the Czechs reluctantly let this small, cheeky foreigner join in. Things go fine for Bill and his confidence begins to return. Their manager orders the Czechs to attack; into the back of the bunch they speed. Bill swerves, dodges and fights his way through to the front. He arrives at last, only to see the rear wheels of the Czechs vanishing in the distance.

KING OF SPORTS

An international stage race in Belgium; Bill and Dick Bartrop are two of the English team and have developed a friendly rivalry to see who will finish the highest on general classification.

This has been a grim day for the English team. Dick crashed early in the stage and has 50 kms. to go. Bill is brought off heavily. By the time he has straightened himself and his machine out, four minutes have passed.

Soon Bill starts in a hopeless pursuit. Looking back down the road, to his delight, he sees a lorry catching him in a large cloud of dust from the dry, dirt road. If Bill can take shelter, he will probably avoid being disqualified for being outside the time limit and would also keep ahead of Dick (he thinks with a chuckle).

Bill changes into top gear and with a huge effort, he accelerates and, choking with the dust, he makes shelter. Alongside him he hears a laugh and to his surprise sees, under several layers of dirt, Dick Bartrop.

We were members of the R.A.F. team for the Isle of Man and a famous food and medicine manufacturer had sent their new, and rather revolutionary dietician to advise us. He told us to eat lots of potatoes, chips, bread and fat which are full of calories, and he assures us energy is made from calories.

The R.A.F. canteen was delighted for these are amongst their favourite, in fact, only dishes. We were plied with stacks of chips, mountains of potatoes, and skyscrapers of fried bread.

The night before the race we had just had a cold shower and were having a rub down in the billet when Bill Baty rushed in, shivering and wet. 'Look lads' he shouted, pointing to his 'goose pimples', 'I've eaten so many calories that they're living out in tents'.

Cycle racing is full of characters like Bill who, when the going is tough, are an asset to any team.

CHAPTER 17

THREE OF MY MOST MEMORABLE EVENTS

THE ISLE OF MAN INTERNATIONAL

I dodge through the doorway into the changing marquee. My excitement rises as I smell the embrocation and orange peel, see the glistening line up of thoroughbred machines and hear the mixture of languages being shouted at groups of Continental riders who have pieces of tape across their sponsors' names on their caps and shorts.

Last minute as usual, but I am used to this, and in ten minutes I am ready as the call goes up for us to line up behind the national flags for the start of the Isle of Man International. The loud-speaker announced the inclusion of reserves and mentions Baldini of Italy, but no one takes any notice because Bruni, the famous Italian, is riding. The England team manager has told his boys that this is the danger man, and stories of his fantastic rides are known to everyone.

The first few miles are hectic, but the bunch settles down just before the first prime. Over the top and the bunch regroups and nearly everyone is feeling like a rest. I attack. Harry Reynolds, Bladon, Holmes and Booty are amongst a few others with the same idea. Over the top of the mountain, we are over a minute ahead. With a great effort Stan Brittain and a Frenchman join us.

We're halfway round the second lap and there are about ten in our group, which is going well, apart from a Frenchman and the Italian, Baldini, who shirks at every opportunity. Shouts of Allez, Tempo, and other expressions unprintable do not produce any favourable results. All the Italian does is look back down the road and mutter 'wait for Bruni'.

The first time I realize the potential of Baldini is the Ramsey town prime, at the bottom of the mountain, on the last lap. Stan makes a last effort to win the prime and two or three riders fight it out with him. Baldini, the others, and I prefer to save our energy for the climb. Then suddenly Baldini gets worried, perhaps thinking that he will not be able to catch the leaders after the sprint. In 200 yards he closes the 50-yard gap the sprinters have opened and nearly beats Stan for the prime.

It is rather late in the race to try and get rid of the lone Continental opposition. Booty would attack and I sit on the Italian's wheel, but when I attack it is one of my own countrymen who closes the gap. Baldini has a comparatively easy ride up the hill. I used to think 98 in. gear was high enough for any descent and said if I couldn't twiddle 98, I could free wheel as fast, but Baldini proves me so wrong. I suffer more hanging on to him down the mountain than all three climbs put together. He has 115 in. gear and his legs are going like bees wings.

Baldini pulls off a great long sprint to win the race. Little did we part-time English cyclists, who had worked twice as hard, realise, that in three years when we were still struggling, this aided amateur would become professional champion of the world.

THE NATIONAL CHAMPIONSHIPS

After my Isle of Man ride Benny Foster, the England team manager, had entered me for the National Championships. The race was on a very hilly circuit in Co. Durham.

It was only when my wife Nora told me we could stay with her aunt in Carlisle and my father lent me his car, that I decided that I could afford to ride.

The race started off in a misty drizzle which lasted for half the event. For the first lap I rode at the back unconcerned, talking to stragglers. After two laps I moved to the front in time to see Dave Tweddell and another England international rider attacking. I went after them; for over half a lap I foolishly chased, but finally lost sight of them in the mist and waited for the bunch. When Dave was finally caught, I asked him why he had not waited. He said that the mist was so thick that he thought the bunch were on my tail. I went to the back of the bunch to recuperate.

Soon afterwards, and before I had recovered, the bunch began to string out, for the long hills were taking their toll. I fought my way to the front and saw the favourite for the race, Allen Jackson, along with several of the top riders, disappearing down the road. A group of riders came flying past me in hot pursuit and with my last effort I accelerated and joined them.

As the distance closed, the hot pace began to tell, and soon there were only two of us and only 15 yards to catch the leaders. Jim Grieves, the other rider, pulled out for me to do 'my bit' at the front, but I was too exhausted and told him so.

THREE OF MY MOST MEMORABLE EVENTS

With a grim look and me hanging on, Jim closed the gap. I felt shocking, I was shattered, my cap had shrunk with the early rain and given me a headache. I saw my wife at the feeding station and shouted to her to get me some aspirins from the car.

Steady bit and bit in the leading group of seven, the sun started shining and I began to recover. Round a bend, and there was Nora and one of the prime judges. I dropped back and the judge handed me the aspirins. I quickly recaught the group and was told, by one of the riders I would get disqualified if I ate them. I was feeling better and sooner than jeopardise my chances I threw them away.

Soon we were climbing again. Jackson and I pulled away from the rest. Suddenly, the chief Judge's car, which had only just caught us pulled alongside us and told me to drop out. I had been disqualified for feeding (the aspirins) outside the feeding zone.

I was shocked. What should I do? Were aspirins food? This was just an event rule not an official rule and a judge had handed them up. The chief judge had not seen the action and therefore received the tale from someone else without hearing my explanation. The rule is intended to stop some dangerous person running into a large bunch to hand someone a drink etc. I had dropped well behind the small group I was in and had not caused the slightest risk to anyone. With these thoughts, and the thought that, if I dropped out and was then found to be innocent it would be too late, I decided to carry on.

Jackson and I kept taking turns at the front, but the judge did not like this, and told Jackson that if he worked with me, he would disqualify him also. Jackson looked at me, and I suggested that we should ride side by side not helping each other. I thought he was tiring and, as I forged ahead, he dropped behind. We came to the last long descent, and I sat up, ate a banana, and had a drink of sherry. Jackson tore past with the chief Judge, Press and other official cars in hot pursuit. Allen Jackson, they thought, was on his way to yet another victory.

I finished my snack and began to overtake the cars. I caught Allen halfway up the last steep climb and attacked. He had no answer. I time trialed the last three miles to the finish. My unjust disqualification was upheld and Allen, who himself finished several minutes in front of the next group, containing most of England's best riders, was National Champion.

KING OF SPORTS
STAGE 5 – THE TOUR OF BRITAIN

I wake. Yes, this is the fifth stage of the Tour of Britain, and by now I sleep like a log. My legs still have a dull ache, but not as bad as the shattered, useless feeling after the first two stages. I slowly rise, have a loosening-up shake and do a couple of Yoga poses, slowly drink a cup of cold water. Clean my teeth etc. Next, I put on my racing clothing and track suit, pack my suitcase and kit bag, gather up my vitamin pills and protein supply and wander down for breakfast. My team manager has arranged for me to have a large piece of grilled gammon for breakfast, as I seem to find steak difficult to eat and digest.

Soon we are riding down to the start, and as we speculate our chances, I check my gears. I am lying fifth on general and feel fine at last. I must have recovered from my strenuous riding on the first two days.

The de-neutralised flag drops and the race is begun in earnest. I am, as usual, close to the front. One or two riders keep jumping away, but the bunch is working smoothly, and they are soon absorbed. The pace slows a little after ten miles and a few riders sneak away individually and join up in front of the bunch. It looks dangerous, so I give chase with the stylish Gil Taylor and young Hughie Porter. After four hard miles we catch the break and are surprised to find it consisting of 12 riders.

The pace is fantastic. It is all I can do to speed past the rider in front and get out of the way for the next rider to do the same. The acceleration required to get behind the last rider as the line comes flashing by nearly tears my legs off. For ten miles the break keeps up the terrific pace. I look back and to my amazement the bunch are right behind. Stretched in a long, thin line, these riders slowly catch us. The grim and sweat-lined faces of our pursuers showed how desperate their chase must have been.

I hear the dreaded noise of compressed air escaping and, to my distress, realise it is my rear tyre. Up goes my hand to signal the service van to my aid. The tyre goes flat so quickly that I can't accelerate to the front, and so I pull into the roadside and start to fuss, removing my rear wheel, when a hand rests on my shoulder and a steady voice says, 'Sit down lad and let my mechanic get on with his job'. I calm down and sit down on the bumper. The mechanic does know his job. He finishes, holds the bike while I change the gear down. I sit in the saddle and ask him to hold me up while I tighten my toe straps – a push and my do or die pursuit is on.

THREE OF MY MOST MEMORABLE EVENTS

Speed, speed, I think, and hope my tired legs will respond. A ray of hope appears on the clouded horizon. Geoff Salter, my teammate, is waiting for me. After a slogging, energy-sapping chase we catch up the ambulance at the rear of the caravan. A short rest, then a sprint to the next team car, rest, sprint, rest, sprint through the convoy. (Some of the team cars slow and pull in, as if I hadn't enough on my plate – these gentlemen will not help). I wind my weary way through the tail end of the field to the relative shelter of the centre of the field.

I have hardly got my breathing back to normal racing tempo when we start a long, hard climb. Halfway up my legs just give up, and gradually the bunch pulls away and I am with the stragglers. At the summit, the bunch are out of sight and I am in no condition to chase on my own, so I look around and slogging up behind me is the huge Czech rider who we nicknamed Garth. I know his strength and weight are ideal for speedy descending. I relax, breathe deeply and wait. Soon Garth comes thundering past. I jump onto his wheel, faster and faster he goes pushing a gear of about 120 inches. The wind comes whipping round Garth, plucking and tugging at me, trying to wrench me away; but I know 'this is my last train home', and I hang on like grim death.

Once more, I wearily wind my way through the tail-end riders to the centre of the bunch. The remaining miles pass slowly. I curse every seemingly fresh rider who starts an attack. I call on my aching legs for extra speed, dreading that the call will not be answered.

Warwick Dalton, the big, strong New Zealander, attacks and pulls away with four riders at six miles to go. With three miles to go as we top Birdlip Hill the sky blackens and down come hail stones as big as marbles. The road becomes a battlefield as riders hurt by the stones slam their brakes on and skid, coming to grief on the wet road. I have suffered so much today that the hail stones don't affect me so much. I keep off my brakes, crouch low and bend my head to protect as much of my bare skin as possible. My speed, combined with the size of the hail stones, causes them to cut my skin and soon my arms and legs are running with blood and water.

I arrive at the bottom, cold, numb and sore, but the hail mercifully stops and, just ahead, I see Dalton and the leading group. Suddenly the pain disappears; with a bit of effort, I am with them. Round the last traffic island and with a quarter of a mile to go, Bill Seggar skids and crashes in front of me. I just ride over him, there's no time to swerve. A policeman says, 'lucky devil', and I think, 'He doesn't know a half of it'. I finish just after Dalton and his group, but in front of the bunch and retain my position on general classification. I am tired but elated. This is stage racing at its toughest, and I have survived.

Peter Ward, front far right, with his father Harry holding Peter's son Dave next to him in the crowd. At that time Peter was the Lakeland Divisional Champion.

PUBLISHER'S NOTE

I discovered *King of Sports* after family friend Cerise Ward, Peter's daughter, posted about it on Facebook a few years ago. I found a copy on eBay, and was absorbed by the powerful content. First and foremost this is an artefact, yet it still feels relevant, even for the weekend cyclist like myself.

Today, the sport is obsessed with tech; Peter's work strips cycling back to the foundations of what it takes to reach your potential on a bike, which isn't the latest gadgets – it's your health, wellbeing and a love for riding. Whether you're a professional racer or casual fan, Ward's revolutionary work will help you understand racing as both an individual and team sport, but also its benefits to one's physical and mental health.

This new version of *King of Sports* has respectfully restored the original illustrations and diagrams without over-producing and retracting from Ward's original work. It was important for us to remain faithful to the 1967 edition whilst ensuring it speaks to the modern cycling enthusiast.

Thank you to the Ward family for all their support and assistance, Brian Cookson for his Foreword and encouragement, and Luke Pajak for his patience and fantastic design.

Sherif Dhaimish, 2024

Director
Pendle Press

KING OF SPORTS
RECOMMENDED BOOKS

HOW TO BECOME A CHAMPION
by Percy Cerutty
published by Stanley Paul

HATHA YOGA
by Yogi Ramacharaka
published by L. N. Fowles & Co.

YOUR DIET IN HEALTH AND DISEASE
by Harry Benjamin
published by Health for All Publishing Co.

MY WORLD ON WHEELS
by Russell Mockeridge
published by Stanley Paul

CYCLING IS MY LIFE
by Tommy Simpson
published by Stanley Paul

WONDER WHEELS
by Eileen Sheridan
published by Nicholas Kaye